.NET Development Using the Compiler API

Jason Bock

Apress®

.NET Development Using the Compiler API

Jason Bock
Shakopee
Minnesota, USA

ISBN-13 (pbk): 978-1-4842-2110-5   ISBN-13 (electronic): 978-1-4842-2111-2
DOI 10.1007/978-1-4842-2111-2

Library of Congress Control Number: 2016945755

Managing Director: Welmoed Spahr
Lead Editor: James DeWolf
Technical Reviewer: Fabio Claudio Ferracchiati
Editorial Board: Steve Anglin, Pramila Balan, Aaron Black, Louise Corrigan, Jonathan Gennick, Robert Hutchinson, Celestin Suresh John, James Markham, Natalie Pao, Susan McDermott, Matthew Moodie, Ben Renow-Clarke, Gwenan Spearing
Coordinating Editor: Melissa Maldonado
Copy Editor: Laura Lawrie
Compositor: SPi Global
Indexer: SPi Global
Artist: SPi Global

Distributed to the book trade worldwide by Springer Science+Business Media New York, 233 Spring Street, 6th Floor, New York, NY 10013. Phone 1-800-SPRINGER, fax (201) 348-4505, e-mail orders-ny@springer-sbm.com, or visit www.springeronline.com. Apress Media, LLC is a California LLC and the sole member (owner) is Springer Science + Business Media Finance Inc (SSBM Finance Inc). SSBM Finance Inc is a **Delaware** corporation.

For information on translations, please e-mail rights@apress.com, or visit www.apress.com.

Apress and friends of ED books may be purchased in bulk for academic, corporate, or promotional use. eBook versions and licenses are also available for most titles. For more information, reference our Special Bulk Sales–eBook Licensing web page at www.apress.com/bulk-sales.

Any source code or other supplementary materials referenced by the author in this text are available to readers at www.apress.com/9781484221105. For detailed information about how to locate your book's source code, go to www.apress.com/source-code/. Readers can also access source code at SpringerLink in the Supplementary Material section for each chapter.

Printed on acid-free paper

Contents at a Glance

Contents

About the Author

Jason Bock is a Practice Lead for Magenic (http://www.magenic.com) and a Microsoft MVP (C#). He has 20 years of experience working on a number of business applications using a diverse set of frameworks and languages such as C#, .NET, and JavaScript. He is the author of *Metaprogramming in .NET*, *Applied .NET Attributes*, and *CIL Programming: Under the Hood of .NET*. He has written numerous articles on software development issues and has presented at a number of conferences and user groups. He is a leader of the Twin Cities Code Camp (http://www.twincitiescodecamp.com). Jason holds a Master's degree in electrical engineering from Marquette University. Visit his website at http://www.jasonbock.net.

About the Technical Reviewer

A prolific writer on cutting-edge technologies, **Fabio Claudio Ferracchiati** has contributed to more than a dozen books on .NET, C#, Visual Basic, and ASP.NET. He is a .NET Microsoft Certified Solution Developer and lives in Milan, Italy. You can read his blog at http://www.Ferracchiati.com.

Acknowledgments

I'd like to thank Apress for contacting me at VSLive in 2015 and asking me if I'd be interested in writing a book on the Compiler API. Getting the opportunity to write on a topic that I've been deeply interested in since I heard about it eight years ago was something I just couldn't pass up. Specifically, I'd like to thank Anne Marie Walker, James DeWolf, Mark Powers, Melissa Maldonado, and Fabio Claudio Ferracchiati for their assistance, guidance, and editing prowess—they made the book far better than it would have been if I did it on my own.

Thanks also to Magenic, especially Greg Frankenfield and Paul Fridman, for creating and growing a great place to work. I've been with Magenic for 15 years, and I feel fortunate to work for a dynamic and innovative company where I fit in. Here's to another 15 (or more!) years. I'd also like to thank Jeff Ferguson for providing a couple of figures for me that are used in the book.

Finally, I'd like to thank my family for their support and encouragement: my wife Liz and my sons Hayden and Ryan. I am grateful to have found someone like Liz and that we've been able to have two awesome sons.

Introduction

Most developers I know typically view coding as a means to an end. That is, they write the code to satisfy the requirements set forth by the business. The code is interpreted or compiled, but either way, the final result is machine code that executes and (hopefully) does the right thing.

However, there's more to software development than just that. I'm not talking about process or patterns per se; what I'm getting at is for developers to view their code in a more analytical way. Throughout my career, I've run into numerous cases in which I would've loved to have the ability to analyze my code so I could find errors quickly. I've also wanted to be able to extend and augment languages in certain ways so I didn't have to write the same code over and over again. The primary language that I've used throughout my career has been C#, and although C# is a fine language to develop in, it seemed to lack these dynamic, analytical capabilities.

That's no longer the case. Microsoft has provided public, open-source components in its Compiler API that allows developers to create analyzers that will help them detect problematic issues. This API also empowers developers to build code at runtime to create amazing, dynamic applications and libraries. Because all of this code is open source, it's available to read and contribute to. Enabling .NET developers to shape and mold the future of the .NET compilation system is a wonderful thing to behold, and it's exciting to see the development community embrace this model.

I wrote this book to help you navigate this new open-source API world. In it, I demonstrate how to use the Compiler API to write custom analyzers and refactorings to improve your code base. I show you how to use the Scripting API (part of the Compiler API) to use C# as a scripting language, a feature that was essentially unavailable to C# developers. I also illustrate how to use the Compiler API in innovative ways that go beyond these typical scenarios. My hope is that when you've finished this book, you'll view C# and the ecosystem that supports it in a fundamentally different (and hopefully positive!) way—as a language that is open in terms of its implementation and its community involvement.

Who This Book Is For

This book is for architects and developers who have experience with C# and want to dive deeper into how code is compiled and executed. There's no expectation that the reader has any experience with compilers, but I do assume that the reader has foundational knowledge of C#.

Chapter Contents

To give you a feel for the content in the book, here's a brief synopsis of each chapter.

- Chapter 1—You'll get an introduction to the Compiler API and its constituent parts: syntax trees, semantic models, and formatters.

- Chapter 2—This chapter covers diagnostics. You'll learn how to write analyzers and build code fixes to automate code corrections.

- Chapter 3—Refactoring code is a primary tenant for developers. This chapter shows you how to write refactorings to clean up your code base.

- Chapter 4—C# is now a scripting language! In this chapter, you'll see how the Scripting API works.

- Chapter 5—You'll discover how developers are using the Compiler API to empower their own components and get a preview of a future C# feature based on the Compiler API that could fundamentally change how you write code in C#.

Code Samples

Throughout the book I show code snippets to illustrate various aspects of the Compiler API. You'll find all of the code at https://github.com/jasonbock/compilerAPIBook. The folder structure is set up to map the code content to each chapter of the book.

Errata

The author, the technical reviewers, and many Apress staff have made every effort to find and eliminate all errors from this book's text and code. Even so, there are bound to be one or two glitches left. To keep you informed, there's an Errata tab on the Apress book page (www.apress.com/9781484221105). If you find any errors that haven't already been reported, such as misspellings or faulty code, please let us know by e-mailing support@apress.com.

Customer Support

Apress wants to hear what you think—what you liked, what you didn't like, and what you think could be done better next time. You can send comments to feedback@apress.com. Be sure to mention the book title in your message.

Contacting the Author

Feel free to follow me on Twitter at @jasonbock. My web site is http://www.jasonbock.net. You can also contact me via e-mail at jasonb@magenic.com.

CHAPTER 1

An Overview of the Compiler API

This chapter covers the basics of the Compiler API, including the essentials of a compiler and their history in the .NET world. You'll learn how to compile code and the trees that constitute the fundamental API data structure. You'll discover how to build your own trees from scratch and navigate their content. Finally, we'll explore annotating and formatting trees.

From Closed to Open

Compilers are used more than any other tool by a developer. Every time you tell Visual Studio to build your code, you're invoking csc.exe, which is the C# compiler. Without compilers, your C# code would be worthless. In this section, you'll gain an understanding of what compilers do, how they've been designed in the .NET world, and how they have changed in .NET 4.6.

Note You can invoke csc.exe directly from the command line, but generally most .NET developers will use it indirectly through Visual Studio or some other IDE.

Electronic supplementary material The online version of this chapter (doi:10.1007/978-1-4842-2111-2_1) contains supplementary material, which is available to authorized users.

© Jason Bock 2016
J. Bock, .NET Development Using the Compiler API, DOI 10.1007/978-1-4842-2111-2_1

What Do Compilers Do?

It's almost a tradition in the developer's world to have a program print "Hello world" to get familiar with the fundamentals of a language, so that's where we'll start our discussion of compilers. Here's code that will do just that:

```
using System;
namespace HelloWorld
{
  class Program
  {
    static void Main(string[] args)
    {
      Console.Out.WriteLine("Hello world");
    }
  }
}
```

Figure 1-1 shows you what you'll see when you run the program.

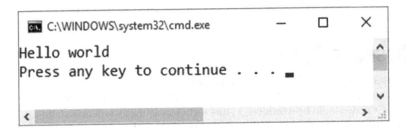

Figure 1-1. *Running a simple Hello World program*

Of course, your computer didn't "execute" that text. There's a translation step that, most of the time, you probably don't think about, and that's what the compiler does. It's easy to say that you've compiled your code, but there's a lot that a compiler has to do to make your code actually execute. Let's do a simplistic examination of a compiler's workflow to get a better understanding of its machinery.

First, the compiler scans your text and figures out all the tokens that are contained within. Tokens are the individual textural pieces within code that have meaning based on a language's specification. These can be member names, language keywords, and operators. For example, Figure 1-2 shows what the line of code that prints out "Hello world" looks like when it's tokenized.

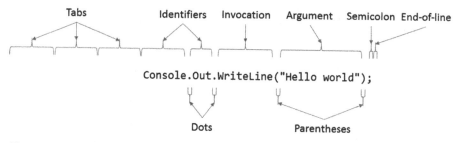

Figure 1-2. Breaking code into separate tokens

The compiler will find *everything* it can about that line of text and break it up into separate chunks. That includes the period between Console and Out, the tabs before the Console token, and the semicolon at the end of the line. The compiler also has to be smart enough to figure out when there are problems and report meaningful errors when its process is finished without stopping on that one error because there may be more issues in the code.

But the complexities of tokenizing code don't stop here. Now the compiler needs to figure out what those tokens really mean. A tab isn't important from an execution standpoint, but it may matter if you're debugging your code, as the compiler needs to make sure the debugging information ignores that whitespace correctly when a developer creates breakpoints in code. A semicolon means that the line of code is complete, so that's important to know, although you're not really doing any execution with that character. But what does the period mean? It may mean that you're trying to access a property on an object, or call a method. Which one is it? And if it's a method, is it an extension method? If so, where does that extension method exist? Is there an appropriate using statement in the file that will help the compiler figure out where that method is? Or is the developer using a new feature in C#6, like using static, which needs to be accounted for? The compiler needs to figure out semantics for these tokens based on the rules of the C# language, and if you've ever read the C# specification, you know that this can be an ·extremely difficult endeavor.

■ **Note**   You'll find the C# specification at https://www.microsoft.com/en-us/download/details.aspx?id=7029, although at the time of this writing, it was at version 5; C#6 features are not included.

Finally, the last job of the compiler is to take all the information it's assembled and actually generate a .NET assembly. This assembly, in turn, contains what's known as an Intermediate Language (IL) that can be interpreted by the Common Language Runtime (CLR) along with metadata information, such as the names of types and methods. Transforming tokens into IL is a nontrivial job. If you've spent any time working with members in the System.Reflection.Emit namespace, you know it's not easy to encode a method correctly. Forget just one IL instruction and you may end up creating an assembly that will crash horribly at runtime.

To summarize, Figure 1-3 demonstrates what a compiler does with code, although keep in mind that this is a rudimentary view of a compiler's internal components.

Figure 1-3. *General steps that a compiler takes to produce executables*

Here's a brief description of each step:

- Parsing finds each token in code and classifies it.
- Semantics provides meaning to each token (e.g., is the token a type name or a language keyword?).
- Emitting produces an executable based on the semantic analysis of the tokens.

Compilers are complex beasts. Whenever I've done a talk on the Compiler API and asked the audience how many people have created and/or worked on a compiler, I rarely see even one hand go up. Most developers do not spend a significant amount of time developing and maintaining a compiler. They might have written one in a college class, but writing compilers is not an activity most developers ever do on a day-to-day basis. Developers are typically more concerned with creating applications for customers. Plus, creating a compiler that handles the specifications of a given programming language is typically difficult. It's a challenge for just two different implementations of a compiler for a language written by two different teams to work exactly the same. Therefore, developers who use a programming language will gravitate to a very small set of compiler implementations to reduce the chances of discrepancies.

■ **Note** If you're interested in learning more about compilers, check out *Modern Compiler Design* (Springer, 2012) at http://www.springer.com/us/book/9781461446989.

Compilers as a Closed Box

In the .NET space, the compiler has been a monolithic executable that did not have any public APIs exposed. Essentially, you give it path information to the files you want to compile (or include as resources in the assembly) and it produces your executable. Figure 1-4 illustrates how this works.

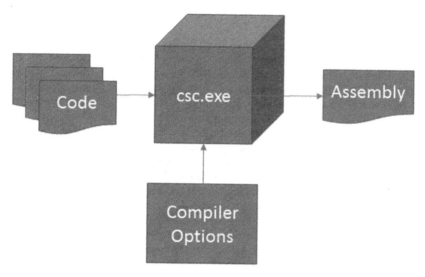

Figure 1-4. *The compiler is a closed box that just does its job*

Notice that you can pass in a handful of optional switches to the compiler to control tasks like optimization (/optimize) and release or debug (/debug) builds. But this interaction is very limited. There's no way to plug into the compiler's pipeline and augment the process, nor can you use any of its functionality outside of compilation.

■ **Note** You can find the latest set of switches for VS2015 at https://msdn.microsoft. com/en-us/library/6ds95cz0.aspx.

Why is this an issue? There are two reasons. First, there are a number of products, both for purchase and open-source, that analyze your code to find issues and suggest refactorings to improve your code's structure and reliability. As discussed in the previous section, parsing and analyzing code is not a trivial endeavor. All of these products and libraries need to invest a fair amount of time duplicating the compilation logic that already exists in the .NET compilers. But they have no choice but to reproduce that functionality as there's no way to access it. This gives rise to the issue of inconsistency. It's possible that the .NET compiler logic and another tool's logic may disagree when it comes to analyzing a specific piece of code. Even if these tools get everything right, whenever a new version of C# comes along with new features, they have to update their code to make sure they're current.

The second reason is that because the compiler is closed, it's harder to build a strong community around it. Traditionally, Microsoft has controlled the compiler's implementation without publishing its source. Although C# is a popular language with millions of developers using it, the community at large hasn't had direct access to its core parts, such as the compiler. There are developers who have a deep interest in being part of that project, either by fixing issues or adding new features to the product. Without an open community, C# developers didn't have a lot of options available to influence the language's direction.

Compilers as an Open Box

Fortunately, Microsoft started working on a new version of the compilers sometime around 2007, using the code name Project Roslyn. This new compiler infrastructure opens up the internals of the pipeline via a public .NET API so anyone can use its functionality within any .NET application. This is a big improvement for tools that provide code analysis as well as for developers who may want to do code generation and dynamic compilation in their own applications. There is now one open standard that everyone can use. Furthermore, as you'll see in Chapters 2 and 3, you can use this API to enhance a .NET developer's experience within Visual Studio via diagnostics and refactorings.

Not only are the compiler assemblies freely available to use, the source code is now available for anyone to read *and* contribute to! On April 4, 2014, Microsoft pushed the entire Compiler API code base to CodePlex. Since then, the project has migrated to GitHub (http://github.com/dotnet/roslyn) with numerous individuals (Microsoft employees and others who don't work for Microsoft) contributing to the code base and providing feedback to various issues and feature requests. This is a major departure from the traditional Microsoft model of closed source. Although Microsoft will always publish "official" versions of the compilers through traditional channels, there's nothing to prevent you from being an active member of this community and contributing to its continuing evolution.

Compiling Code

Having an open source compiler for C# is exciting news, but where do we start? How can you use the compiler's assemblies? In this section you'll get an introduction into the Compiler API. You'll create a C# project that references the Compiler API assemblies, and then you'll use them to compile code on the fly.

Referencing Assemblies

Let's start by creating a project that references the Compiler API assemblies from NuGet so we can build and execute a Hello World application. For the rest of the book, I won't go through these explicit steps of project creation and setup, especially as all of the code samples are online, but this one time I'll walk through it so you know exactly what needs to be done. Create a console application, making sure that the .NET Framework version is 4.6.1, as shown in Figure 1-5.

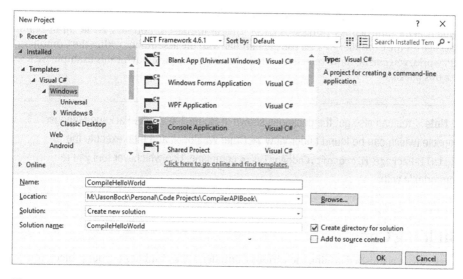

Figure 1-5. *Creating a project that will reference the Compiler API assemblies*

Now, go to the Solution Explorer. Right-click on the References node, and select Manage NuGet Packages. Select Browse, and type in "Microsoft.CodeAnalysis". You should see a list that looks something like the one in Figure 1-6.

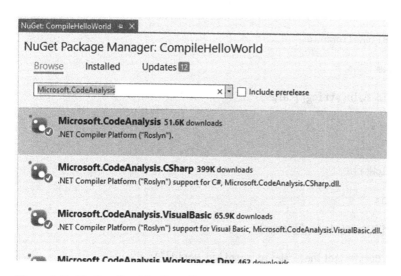

Figure 1-6. *Finding the right Compiler API NuGet package*

Select the "Microsoft.CodeAnalysis" package and install the latest stable version (which, at the time of this writing, was 1.1.1). This, as the description says, is the "all-in-one" package for the Compiler API. As you get familiar with the assemblies within the Compiler API world, you can be more selective with the package you pick, but for this example we'll use this package.

■ **Note** You can also get the packages shown in Figure 1-6 via the Package Manager Console (which can be found under View ➤ Other Windows) and then execute the `Install-Package Microsoft.CodeAnalysis` command. Use whichever tool you're comfortable with.

Building Code

Once NuGet is finished adding the various Compiler API assemblies to your project, you can see how the basics work. Change the Program.cs file so that it looks like Listing 1-1.

Listing 1-1. Compiling a "Hello World" application

```
using Microsoft.CodeAnalysis;
using Microsoft.CodeAnalysis.CSharp;
using System.IO;
using System.Reflection;

namespace CompileHelloWorld
{
  class Program
  {
    static void Main(string[] args)
    {
      var code =
@"using System;

namespace HelloWorld
{
  class Program
  {
    static void Main(string[] args)
    {
      Console.Out.WriteLine(""Hello compiled world"");
    }
  }
}";
```

8

```
var tree = SyntaxFactory.ParseSyntaxTree(code);
var compilation = CSharpCompilation.Create(
  "HelloWorldCompiled.exe",
  options: new CSharpCompilationOptions(
    OutputKind.ConsoleApplication),
  syntaxTrees: new[] { tree },
  references: new[]
  {
    MetadataReference.CreateFromFile(
      typeof(object).Assembly.Location)
  });

using (var stream = new MemoryStream())
{
  var compileResult = compilation.Emit(stream);
  var assembly = Assembly.Load(stream.GetBuffer());
  assembly.EntryPoint.Invoke(null,
    BindingFlags.NonPublic | BindingFlags.Static,
    null, new object[] { null }, null);
}
        }
      }
    }
}
```

Let's go through this code in detail. The code variable is a string that contains the code you want to compile. In this case, it's the same code you saw in the "Hello World" example at the beginning of this chapter, except with a slightly different "Hello" message. We need to parse this code, so that's what ParseSyntaxTree() does (syntax trees will be covered in greater detail in the "Creating Code Using Trees" section later in this chapter). Once we have a tree, we can compile that tree using a CSharpCompilation object, which we get from calling Compile(). Notice that we can specify that this compilation should produce a console application (the OutputKind value), and that it needs to reference the assembly that System.Object comes from (MetadataReference.CreateFromFile()). If this code was referencing types from other assemblies, those MetadataReference objects should be passed into Compile() as well.

The last step is to emit the assembly. Notice that the assembly isn't actually written to disk because we're using a MemoryStream rather than a file-based stream. You can also pass in other streams to capture debug and resource information related to the assembly if you'd like. Once the assembly is created, it's a simple matter of using the EntryPoint property to get access to Main() and invoke it. Figure 1-7 shows what you should see when you run this program.

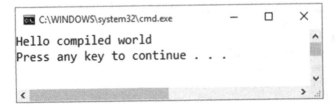

Figure 1-7. *Running code that compiles code at runtime*

■ **Note** As you can see in Listing 1-1, the Compiler API usually has a fair amount of types, method overloads, and optional arguments. In fact, the Microsoft.CodeAnalysis.dll assembly has 246 types and over 23,000 methods! Going through every possible option in this book would be extremely counterproductive; you are highly encouraged to do your own spelunking and explore the numerous types and members that the Compiler API has.

This was a quick introduction into the Compiler API. Now let's take a closer look at trees, the main data structure the Compiler API uses.

Creating Code Using Trees

In the previous section, you saw how you could change text into executable code via the Compiler API. One of the major components of that process was creating a tree. Let's take a deeper dive into what this structure is and how it works. We'll start by using tools that help you see what a tree looks like and how it is composed.

Visualizing Trees

Most developers know what a tree structure is. It starts with one object that contains a list of objects, where those objects can also contain lists of objects, and so on. If you wanted to represent a simple mathematical function, F(a), that performs a calculation like "2 * a" as a tree, you'd probably do it using a similar tree to the one in Figure 1-8.

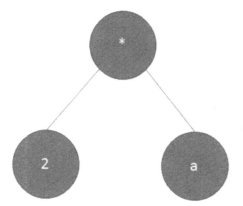

Figure 1-8. *Modeling the "2 * a" function as a tree*

In this case, what the tree represents is easy to see. The "*" node is multiplication, the "2" node is the constant value 2, and the "a" node is the argument to the fuction. Of course, the code we all write is far more complex than that. The trees in the Compiler API that derive from code we'd usually write will never be as small as the tree in Figure 1-8. As Figure 1-9 illustrates, these trees can get quite large.

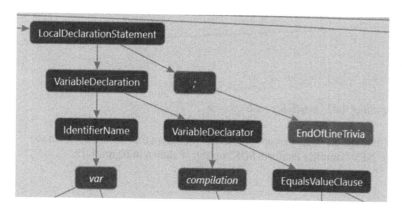

Figure 1-9. *A small part of a tree*

The tree in Figure 1-9 is a very small fragment of the code used in Listing 1-1. Figure 1-10 shows the entire tree for that code.

Figure 1-10. *The full code tree*

11

Even with a small piece of C# code, the tree can get so large you can't even read any of the descriptions for any of the nodes!

Now, you may be wondering how the diagrams in Figure 1-9 and 1-10 were created. It's a tool that comes with the installation of the .NET Compiler SDK that you'll really want to install if you're going to work with the Compiler APIs. Let's make sure you have the required set of tools installed on your machine so you'll be able to generate this diagram if you want as well as build other components discussed in other chapters in this book. To do this, act like you'll create a new project form the Extensibility node (even though you won't), and you should see an option in the list called "Install Visual Studio Extensibility Tools" as illustrated in Figure 1-11.

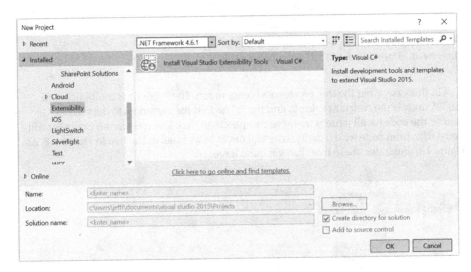

Figure 1-11. *Installing the Extensibility tools*

Second, go thorough the same project creation steps, except this time you should see a "Download the .NET Compiler Platform SDK" option as shown in Figure 1-12.

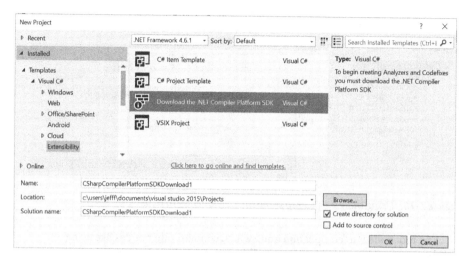

Figure 1-12. *Installing the Compiler Platform SDK*

▓ **Note** Unfortunately, this second step *will* create a project that is worthless. To circumvent this unnecessary project creation step, you can try to download the SDK directly by going to http://go.microsoft.com/fwlink/?LinkID=526901.

In subsequent chapters we'll use the project templates that are installed by performing these steps, but for now we'll just use one extremely useful window that should have been added in Visual Studio after you installed these tools. Select View ➤ Other Windows to see an option for Syntax Visualizer.

▓ **Note** You can also use Quick Launch (Ctrl+Q) to search for and access Syntax Visualizer. Ctrl+Q is one of the most powerful keystrokes you can use in Visual Studio as it can find any command in the product, while also showing you if there's a key mapping for that tool. If you haven't used it before, I highly recommend getting familiar with it.

The Syntax Visualizer makes it easy to see what the full tree looks like for a given piece of code in Visual Studio. Figure 1-13 is a screenshot of the Visualizer in action.

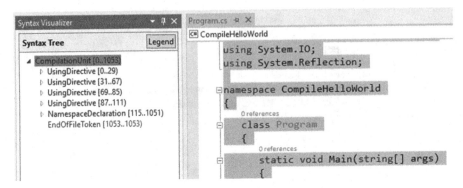

Figure 1-13. Using the Visualizer to show the tree for code in a file

The root node is a "compilation unit," which contains other nodes like using directives and a namespace declaration. (I'll cover the specific types later in this section.) If you click on a specific member in your code, the tree will expand to that exact node in the tree. In Figure 1-14, the focus has been moved to the declaration of the Program class.

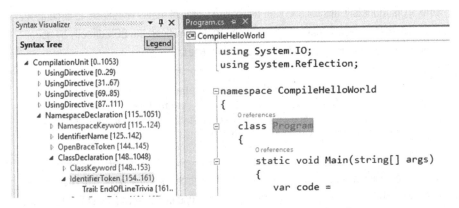

Figure 1-14. Highlighting a specific piece of code to move around in the tree

We'll get to what the types mean shortly. For now, notice that the Syntax Visualizer moved to the node in the tree that represents the name of the class—an IdentifierTokenNode, which is part of a ClassDeclaractionSyntax node.

The tree will also work if you have errors in your code, which demonstrates how hard the Compiler APIs work to give you a tree with as much information as possible. Figure 1-15 shows what the tree looks like if you remove the opening curly brace after the namespace declaration.

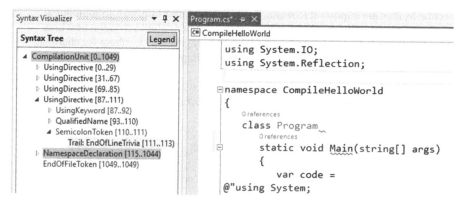

Figure 1-15. *The Syntax Visualizer with errors in the code*

You can see that the tree starts highlighting certain nodes with a pink rectangle to illustrate that there are errors within. You may not be able to see the pink highlighting color if you're viewing this in grayscale, but it's there onscreen. The Legend button shows what each color in the tree represents, as you can see in Figure 1-16.

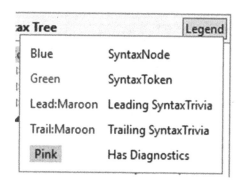

Figure 1-16. *The color coding in the Syntax Visualizer*

Up to now I've been using the word "node" in a generic fashion to talk about the members within a tree, but it's time to get a little more formal about the types within a Compiler API tree. There are essentially three base types: SyntaxNode, SyntaxToken, and SyntaxTrivia. SyntaxNode is an abstract class that can contain other tree types (either directly or indirectly). Specific kinds of SyntaxNode classes are ClassDeclarationSyntax, which specifies the contents of a class, and ParameterListSyntax, which defines the parameters for a methd. A SyntaxToken is a struct that defines a termination in the tree and is used to specify items like keywords, idenifiers, braces, and so on. The different kinds of tokens are represented by the Kind property, which is a SyntaxKind enumeration value. SyntaxTrivia are also structs, and they make up all the "unimportant" parts of code, like spaces, tabs and end-of-line characters. Although they don't affect the resultant executable, they are important to retain. To prove how important, go into someone's code, and if they put the opening curly brace to a member definition on the next line, move it to the end of the previous line. You'll definitely get some feedback for changing that coding style! We'll focus on preserving trivia in Chapters 2 and 3 when we change code for a developer to improve their applications.

Finally, if you want to create the diagram in Figure 1-10, simply right-click on any node within the Visualizer, and select View Directed Syntax Graph. Figure 1-17 shows this context menu.

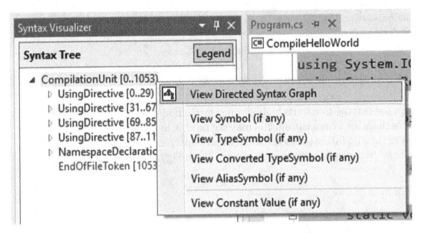

Figure 1-17. Using the Syntax Visualizer to print a pretty tree diagram of your code

The Syntax Visualizer is a tool that you'll probably end up using a lot as you wade through the Compiler API because it makes it easy to find out what nodes constitute a specific part of the C# language. For example, an IdentifierTokenNode does what its name implies: it identifies a node within a tree. As you've seen in Figures 1-13, 1-14, and 1-15, the Syntax Visualizer shows the names of the node kinds, like CompilationUnit and NamespaceDeclaration. The node's type name appears in the Properties section of the Syntax Visualizer, as shown in Figure 1-18.

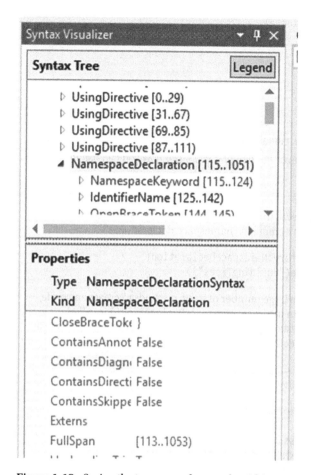

Figure 1-18. Seeing the type name for a node within a tree

The Syntax Visualizer is great for finding out which parts of your code map to what types in the Compiler API. All you have to do is type some code in Visual Studio, and the visualizer automatically shows you everything you need to see in a tree. But how can you create and manipulate the tree structure itself? That's what we'll do in the next section.

Building Trees

In this section, we'll create a tree from scratch. We'll use the example of the "2 * a" function mentioned in the previous section and turn that into a C# method:

```
namespace BuildingTrees
{
  public static class Doubler
  {
```

```
public static int Double(int a)
{
  return 2 * a;
}
}
}
```

■ **Note**   In C# you can't just write a small piece of code like "2 * a"; you need a method declaration along with a class. However, in Chapter 4 you'll see how you can use the Scripting APIs to do just that!

To create a tree that will represent this code, you'll use the SyntaxFactory class along with the SyntaxTree class. First, let's create the namespace declaration:

```
var treeNamespace = SyntaxFactory.NamespaceDeclaration(
  SyntaxFactory.IdentifierName("BuildingTrees"))
```

The SyntaxFactory class has a large number of static methods to create any node, token, or trivia you need in a tree. In this case, NamespaceDeclaration() is called, passing in the IdentifierNameSyntax object creatd from IdentifierName() to create a NamespaceDeclarationSyntax object.

Next, create a class:

```
var doublerClass = SyntaxFactory.ClassDeclaration("Doubler");
```

Then add the Double method to that class:

```
var doubleMethod = doublerClass.WithMembers(
  SyntaxFactory.SingletonList<MemberDeclarationSyntax>(
    SyntaxFactory.MethodDeclaration(
      SyntaxFactory.PredefinedType(
        SyntaxFactory.Token(
          SyntaxKind.IntKeyword)),
        SyntaxFactory.Identifier("Double"))));
```

Notice that with a MethodDeclarationSyntax, you need to define the return type, which, with Double() is an int. That's why PredefinedType() is called, using SyntaxKind. IntKeyword as "int" is already known in the C# type system.

To actually create the entire CompilationUnitSyntax object that contains all of the nodes, tokens, and trivia takes a fair amount of code. It's also quite repetitive in nature. If you want to see the entire tree, you'll find it in the BuildingTrees project for this chapter. Keep in mind that the code wasn't generated by hand. There's a wonderful tool that you can use that generates a CompilationUnitSyntax for you based on a C# code snippet called RoslynQuoter. You can get the code for the RoslynQuoter tool at https://github.com/KirillOsenkov/RoslynQuoter, but there's an online version of it at http://roslynquoter.azurewebsites.net/. Figure 1-19 shows what this website looks like.

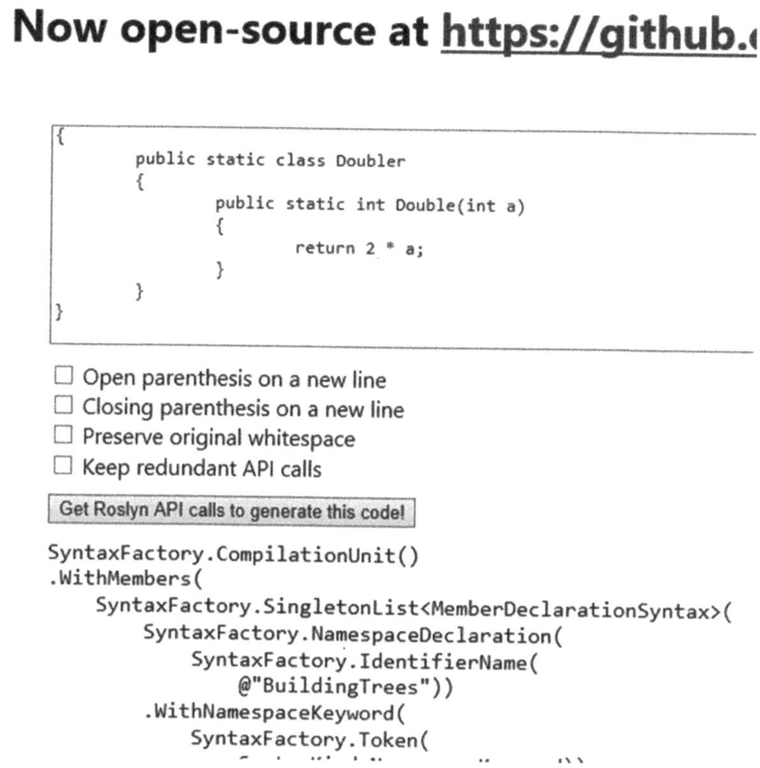

Now open-source at https://github.

```
{
    public static class Doubler
    {
        public static int Double(int a)
        {
            return 2 * a;
        }
    }
}
```

- ☐ Open parenthesis on a new line
- ☐ Closing parenthesis on a new line
- ☐ Preserve original whitespace
- ☐ Keep redundant API calls

`Get Roslyn API calls to generate this code!`

```
SyntaxFactory.CompilationUnit()
.WithMembers(
    SyntaxFactory.SingletonList<MemberDeclarationSyntax>(
        SyntaxFactory.NamespaceDeclaration(
            SyntaxFactory.IdentifierName(
                @"BuildingTrees"))
        .WithNamespaceKeyword(
            SyntaxFactory.Token(
```

Figure 1-19. *Using RoslynQuoter to generate syntax trees*

The lines of code to generate the CompilationUnitSyntax object is around 100. That's a lot! But once you have that root node, you can put it into a tree:

```
var tree = SyntaxFactory.SyntaxTree(unit);
```

Once the tree is created, you can compile that tree and invoke the method, as shown in Listing 1-2.

Listing 1-2. Compiling a syntax tree

```
var compilation = CSharpCompilation.Create(
  "Doubler.dll",
  options: new CSharpCompilationOptions(
    OutputKind.DynamicallyLinkedLibrary),
  syntaxTrees: new[] { tree },
  references: new[]
```

```
{
    MetadataReference.CreateFromFile(
            typeof(object).Assembly.Location)
});

using (var stream = new MemoryStream())
{
    var compileResult = compilation.Emit(stream);
    var assembly = Assembly.Load(stream.GetBuffer());

    var type = assembly.GetType(
        $"{Program.NamespaceName}.{Program.ClassName}");
    var method = type.GetMethod(Program.MethodName);

    var result = (int)method.Invoke(null, new object[] { 2 });

    Console.Out.WriteLine(result);
}
```

Figure 1-20 shows what you should see when you pass 2 into the Double() method.

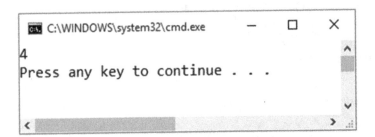

Figure 1-20. *Dynamically invoking a method compiled at runtime*

Now you know how to create trees from scratch. But how can you navigate their content and change what they contain? That's what we'll cover in the next section.

Navigating and Editing Trees

In the previous section, you saw how to create a tree. But what if you're given a tree that you didn't create? You may want to find out what's in it and potentially change it. In this section, we'll cover a couple of different ways you can do that via node methods and classes called walkers. We'll also see what semantic models can do to make tree traversal easier. Finally, you'll discover how to edit these trees to create a new tree. This information is critical to understand when we cover diagnostics in Chapter 2 and refactorings in Chapter 3, so make sure you're comfortable with these concepts before you move on to the content in those chapters.

Finding Content from a Node

Using trees created for you is something you'll do a lot if you're using the Compiler API. As you've already seen, these trees are rich with information. When you run Listing 1-3, you'll see that the resultant tree has nearly 60 items within it:

Listing 1-3. Getting a count of all nodes in a tree

```
var code = @"
using System;

public class ContainsMethods
{
  public void Method1() { }
  public void Method2(int a, Guid b) { }
  public void Method3(string a) { }
  public void Method4(ref string a) { }
}";

var tree = SyntaxFactory.ParseSyntaxTree(code);
Console.Out.WriteLine(
  tree.GetRoot().DescendantNodesAndTokensAndSelf(
    _ => true, true).Count());
```

There's a couple of "Descendant" methods that you can use on a node to find information within it. Listing 1-4 uses DescendantNodes() to find all the methods within that tree.

Listing 1-4. Using DescendantNodes() to find methods

```
private static void PrintMethodContentViaTree(SyntaxTree tree)
{
  var methods = tree.GetRoot().DescendantNodes(_ => true)
    .OfType<MethodDeclarationSyntax>();

  foreach (var method in methods)
  {
    var parameters = new List<string>();

    foreach (var parameter in method.ParameterList.Parameters)
    {
      parameters.Add(
        $"{parameter.Type.ToFullString().Trim()} {parameter.Identifier.Text}");
    }

    Console.Out.WriteLine(
      $"{method.Identifier.Text}({string.Join(", ", parameters)})");
  }
}
```

Figure 1-21 shows what you'll see when you run the code in Listing 1-4.

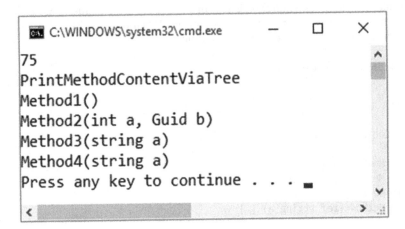

Figure 1-21. Using DescendentNodes() to find method content

Note that although it looks like you're getting type information back as "int" and "Guid" in the console window, the trees don't have that type information available. All a tree has is knowledge about the textural content of the tree's information and how that content relates to C#. You'll see how you can get closer to that type information in the upcoming "Semantic Models" section, but first let's look at another way you can peruse a node's content.

Finding Content Using Walkers

You can use a "walker" class in the Compiler API to discover the information on a tree. For example, the CSharpSyntaxWalker class is a visitor class that will start with a given node and visit every node within that node's tree. Listing 1-5 shows how you can write a class to visit methods in a node, just like what you saw in Listing 1-4.

Listing 1-5. Using a walker to find methods in a tree

```
public sealed class MethodWalker
   : CSharpSyntaxWalker
{
  public MethodWalker(SyntaxWalkerDepth depth = SyntaxWalkerDepth.Node)
    : base(depth)
  { }

  public override void VisitMethodDeclaration(MethodDeclarationSyntax node)
  {
    var parameters = new List<string>();
```

```
    foreach (var parameter in node.ParameterList.Parameters)
    {
      parameters.Add(
        $"{parameter.Type.ToFullString().Trim()} {parameter.Identifier.Text}");
    }

    Console.Out.WriteLine(
      $"{node.Identifier.Text}({string.Join(", ", parameters)})");

    base.VisitMethodDeclaration(node);
  }
}
```

You can override the "Visit" method that matches the kind of content you're looking for. In this case, we want to find method defintions, so we override VisitMethodDeclaration(). The code is essentially the same as what you saw with DescendantNodes() in Listing 1-4, with the same results. So, when should you use one over the other? Using the methods on the node works well if you just want to find one kind of node. You also don't have to create a new class to do that. The walker is advantageous if you want to find multiple node kinds in the tree, as you'll walk it once. Doing that with the node methods can be more cumbersome. Experiment with both and see which one works best with the problem at hand.

In either case, you're still working with nodes and tokens. If you want more information about the tree's content, you'll need to get semantic information, which we'll cover in the next section.

Semantic Models

If you were trying to find crucial information in a node and all you had were the traversal tools described in the previous sections, you'd get frustrated pretty quickly. The nodes have a lot of information, but it's not always obvious how they relate to one another, especially as it pertains to C# and .NET information. For example, what are the type names? Is a class sealed? Is this argument by reference? You could try and piece all of that information together with the nodes, or you can use the semantic model. A semantic model provides a layer on top of the tree to provide a level of information you can't easily stitch together from syntax.

To get a model, you need to use a compilation object like the one in Listing 1-6.

Listing 1-6. Using a semantic model to discover method information

```
private static void PrintMethodContentViaSemanticModel(SyntaxTree tree)
{
  Console.Out.WriteLine(nameof(Program.PrintMethodContentViaSemanticModel));
  var compilation = CSharpCompilation.Create(
    "MethodContent",
    syntaxTrees: new[] { tree },
    references: new[]
```

```
{
  MetadataReference.CreateFromFile(typeof(object).Assembly.Location)
});

var model = compilation.GetSemanticModel(tree, true);

var methods = tree.GetRoot().DescendantNodes(_ => true)
  .OfType<MethodDeclarationSyntax>();

foreach (var method in methods)
{
  var methodInfo = model.GetDeclaredSymbol(method) as IMethodSymbol;
  var parameters = new List<string>();

  foreach (var parameter in methodInfo.Parameters)
  {
    var isRef = parameter.RefKind == RefKind.Ref ? "ref " : string.Empty;
    parameters.Add($"{isRef}{parameter.Type.Name} {parameter.Name}");
  }

  Console.Out.WriteLine(
    $"{methodInfo.Name}({string.Join(", ", parameters)})");
}
}
```

To get method symbol information, you use `GetDeclaredSymbol()` on a semantic tree obtained from the `CSharpCompilation` object. You then cast that to an `IMethodSymbol`, and use that to print out method information as shown in Figure 1-22, which looks exactly the same as Figure 1-21.

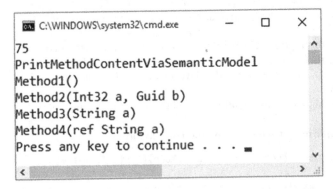

Figure 1-22. *Using a semantic model to find method content*

Note that in this case, we can use the RefKind property to easily figure out if the parameter is passed by reference. To do this with a syntax tree, you'd have to look to see if the descendents of a ParameterSyntax object contains a SyntaxToken that is of a RefKeyword kind. It's doable, but the semantic model makes it easier to find that out.

Also, keep in mind that obtaining a semantic tree requires the compilation object to perform extra work to assemble it. If you run the NavigatingTrees project in the Chapter1 folder from the book's source code repository, you'll see a brief pause when the code gets the semantic model. The model is handy to have around as it makes discovery a much easier endeavor with usually less code, but that comes with a small performance price. You'll have to weigh the cost between the two depending on your scenario.

Now you know how to peruse a tree and find out different aspects about it. But what if you want to change the tree? We'll cover that in the next section.

Editing Trees

In Chapters 2 and 3, you'll need to change the code that a developer has entered to either fix it or refactor it. This requires modifying a tree. However, let's be clear: you don't modify trees in the Compiler API because they're immutable. If you call a method to replace a node in the tree, you get a new node back. The original node's child content hasn't change; the node you got back as a return value is the one with the changes. This may seem like a fairly large memory footprint to deal with all in the name of immutability, but you gain a lot by having immutable structures, like the ability to easily compare between the two nodes in Visual Studio (you'll see this in Chapters 2 and 3). Plus, the size of the memory footprint doesn't double the working set of your process every time you modify a new node. The Compiler API team has worked hard to ensure that the performance and memory footprint of the compiler is efficient.

■ **Note**   If you want a deep dive into the inner workings of trees and how they work with reducing memory pressure, read the article at http://robinsedlaczek.com/2015/04/29/inside-the-net-compiler-platform-performance-considerations-during-syntax-analysis-speakroslyn/.

Let's explore two different ways you can get a "modified" tree back in the Compiler API: replace methods and rewriters. Let's say that you want to change all of the methods in a class so they're public. Listing 1-7 contains the starting tree.

Listing 1-7. Building the source tree

```
var code = @"
using System;

public class ContainsMethods
{
  public void Method1() { }
  protected void Method2(int a, Guid b) { }
  internal void Method3(string a) { }
  private void Method4(ref string a) { }
  protected internal void Method5(long a) { }
}";

var tree = SyntaxFactory.ParseSyntaxTree(code);
```

To change the contents of the node from Listing 1-7 via a replace method, you can use the ReplaceNodes() method, as shown in Listing 1-8.

Listing 1-8. Replacing nodes in a tree via ReplaceNodes()

```
private static void ModifyTreeViaTree(SyntaxTree tree)
{
  Console.Out.WriteLine(nameof(Program.ModifyTreeViaTree));
  Console.Out.WriteLine(tree);
  var methods = tree.GetRoot().DescendantNodes(_ => true)
    .OfType<MethodDeclarationSyntax>();

  var newTree = tree.GetRoot().ReplaceNodes(methods, (method,
  methodWithReplacements) =>
    {
    var visibilityTokens = method.DescendantTokens(_ => true)
      .Where(_ => _.IsKind(SyntaxKind.PublicKeyword) ||
        _.IsKind(SyntaxKind.PrivateKeyword) ||
        _.IsKind(SyntaxKind.ProtectedKeyword) ||
        _.IsKind(SyntaxKind.InternalKeyword)).ToImmutableList();

    if (!visibilityTokens.Any(_ => _.IsKind(SyntaxKind.PublicKeyword)))
      {
      var tokenPosition = 0;

      var newMethod = method.ReplaceTokens(visibilityTokens,
        (_, _) =>
        {
        tokenPosition++;

        return tokenPosition == 1 ?
          SyntaxFactory.Token(
            _.LeadingTrivia,
            SyntaxKind.PublicKeyword,
            _.TrailingTrivia) :
```

```
            new SyntaxToken();
        });
        return newMethod;
    }
    else
    {
        return method;
    }
});

Console.Out.WriteLine(newTree);
}
```

There's a lot going on in Listing 1-8, so let's go through it step by step. Once we get a list of MethodDeclarationSyntax nodes, we call ReplaceNodes(). In this overload, we pass in the list of methods we want to replace, and then a Func that takes two arguments and returns a MethodDeclarationSyntax object. In our implementation, we'll only look at the first argument, as that is a reference to an element that you may want to replace. In the Func, we look for tokens with DescendantTokens() that represent the visibility of the method. If none of them are a "public" token, then we replace the visibility tokens via ReplaceTokens(). The first token in the list is changed to a "public" token, and the rest are removed with a new SyntaxToken()—this effectively gets rid of the token from the tree. Note that we keep the leading and trailing trivia around the first node so we don't lose what the developer has put in the code to format it they way they want it to be.

Figure 1-23 shows what the tree looks like before and after the modification.

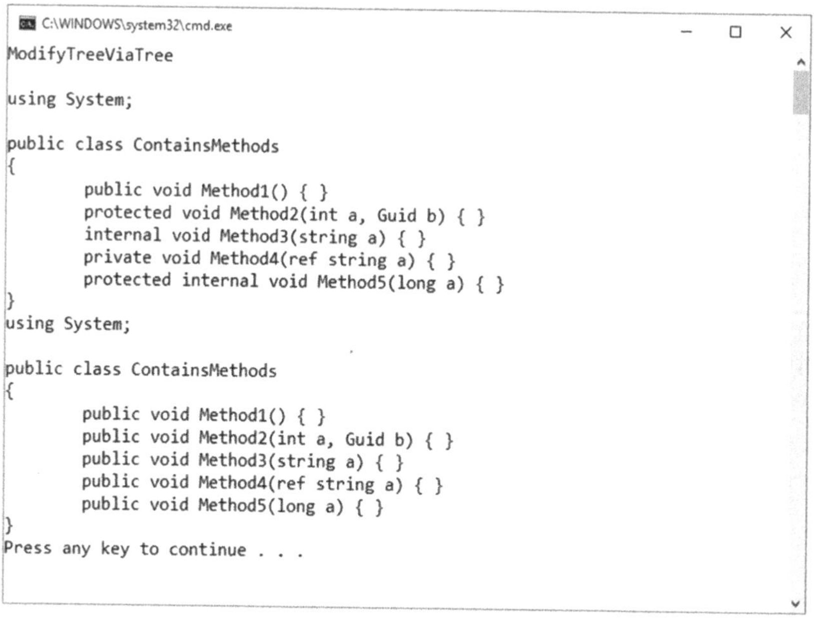

```
C:\WINDOWS\system32\cmd.exe                    —  □  ×
ModifyTreeViaTree

using System;

public class ContainsMethods
{
        public void Method1() { }
        protected void Method2(int a, Guid b) { }
        internal void Method3(string a) { }
        private void Method4(ref string a) { }
        protected internal void Method5(long a) { }
}
using System;

public class ContainsMethods
{
        public void Method1() { }
        public void Method2(int a, Guid b) { }
        public void Method3(string a) { }
        public void Method4(ref string a) { }
        public void Method5(long a) { }
}
Press any key to continue . . .
```

Figure 1-23. Modifying a tree with replacement methods on nodes

27

Remember that the original tree has not changed. All of the work in this code has only created a new tree with new nodes.

As always, there are lots of other methods you can use to replace content, like ReplaceTrivia(), so depending upon your scenario, take a look at the SyntaxNode you have and see if a different "Replace" method matches your needs.

You can also use a visitor class to rewrite the node. You inherit from the CSharpSyntaxRewriter class and override the correct "Visit" methods you need to create a new node. Listing 1-9 shows what a rewriter looks like to make all methods public.

Listing 1-9. Replacing nodes in a tree via a rewriter class

```
public sealed class MethodRewriter
  : CSharpSyntaxRewriter
{
  public override SyntaxNode VisitMethodDeclaration(MethodDeclarationSyntax node)
  {
    var visibilityTokens = node.DescendantTokens(_ => true)
      .Where(_ => _.IsKind(SyntaxKind.PublicKeyword) ||
        _.IsKind(SyntaxKind.PrivateKeyword) ||
        _.IsKind(SyntaxKind.ProtectedKeyword) ||
        _.IsKind(SyntaxKind.InternalKeyword)).ToImmutableList();

    if (!visibilityTokens.Any(_ => _.IsKind(SyntaxKind.PublicKeyword)))
    {
      var tokenPosition = 0;

      var newMethod = node.ReplaceTokens(visibilityTokens,
        (_, _) =>
        {
          tokenPosition++;

          return tokenPosition == 1 ?
            SyntaxFactory.Token(
              _.LeadingTrivia,
              SyntaxKind.PublicKeyword,
              _.TrailingTrivia) :
            new SyntaxToken();
        });
      return newMethod;
    }
    else
    {
      return node;
    }
  }
}
```

Using the rewriter to get a new node is pretty simple:

```
var newTree = new MethodRewriter().Visit(tree.GetRoot());
```

As with reading nodes, the approach you use to create new nodes is up to you.

Before we close out this chapter, let's look at two more pieces of a tree that you may find useful when you create and/or modify trees: annotations and formatters.

Annotations and Formatters

You've seen the core parts of trees that the Compiler API uses throughout its pipeline. But there are two parts to the tree that, while they may not be highly important to the resulting compilation output, you (and those who read the code generated by a tree) may find them useful. They are annotations and formatters. Let's start with annotations.

Using Annotations

Being a .NET developer means you've probably used attributes in some capacity. For example, if you use a unit testing framework, you typically mark a method that should be run as a test with some kind of attribute, like this:

```
[TestMethod]
public void MyTest() { /*...*/ }
```

The TestMethodAttribute is a piece of metadata in your code that lies dormant until code looks for the existence of that attribute and reacts accordingly. In this unit testing example, a test runner would use Reflection to find all methods marked with TestMethodAttribute and invoke them during a test run.

In the Compiler API, you can use an instance of the SyntaxAnnotation class to mark nodes and tokens with a piece of information you'd like to use later on. The annotations won't do anything when the code is compiled; they're only there for you to find and perform some specfic action based on their existence. For example, if you wanted to know how many methods were changed to public based on code from Listing 1-8, you can add an annotation to the new MethodDeclarationSyntax object like this:

```
const string newMethodAnnotation = "MethodMadePublic";

// ... method rewriting goes here ...

return newMethod.WithAdditionalAnnotations(
  new SyntaxAnnotation(newMethodAnnotation));
```

Then you only need one line of code to get the count of changed methods from a tree:

```
newTree.GetAnnotatedNodes(newMethodAnnotation).Count();
```

Annotations are not required for anything you do when you work with trees. In fact, they won't show up when you print code or save it to a text file, nor will they end up in a resulting executable. But they can come in handy when you want to tag elements in a tree to quickly find them later. Speaking of printing code, let's now look at how you can format your code (and, interestingly enough, use an annotation to specify formatting).

Using Formatters

As mentioned earlier in the "Visualizing Trees" section, developers can be really picky about the code they write when it comes to formatting. If they want the curly brace on the next line, they write this:

```
public class MyClass
{
  // ...
}
```

But if someone comes along and changes it to this:

```
public class MyClass {
  // ...
}
```

stern words may be spoken to the one who made the change! How you format your code makes no difference in the way the code will execute when it's compiled, but having consistency pervasive in a code base is one indication that the development team is striving for clean, healthy code.

One way to handle formatting is to explicity add in all the trivia manually. With the RoslynQuoter tool mentioned earlier in the "Building Trees" section, you may have noticed that you had the option to "Preserve original whitespace". If you use that option, all of the nodes created from SyntaxFactory have explicit leading and trailing trivia lists defined. If you omit that option, then the code is less verbose, but it does have a call to NormalizeWhitespace() at the end of the factory calls.

What does NormalizeWhitespace() do? Essentially it applies some "common" C# formatting to the code represented in the tree. For example, consider the code in Listing 1-10.

Listing 1-10. Creating a ClassDeclarationNode

```
public static class Program
{
  public static void Main(string[] args)
  {
    Program.FormatClassNode();
  }
```

```
  private static void FormatClassNode()
  {
    Console.Out.WriteLine(nameof(Program.FormatClassNode));
    var code = SyntaxFactory.ClassDeclaration("NewClass");
    Console.Out.WriteLine(code);
    Console.Out.WriteLine(code.NormalizeWhitespace());
  }
}
```

Here's the output when the code from Listing 1-10 is run:

```
FormatClassNode
classNewClass{}
class NewClass
{
}
```

Notice that the second line is the class definition with no formatting, and the last two lines are the definition with formatting applied. You can use overloads of NormalizeWhitespace() to define the indentation and end-of-line trivia if you'd like, but that's it—you have to use whatever formatting NormalizeWhitespace() decides to apply.

You can also use workspaces to define how the tree's code should be formatted. We'll cover workspaces in detail in Chapter 4, but for now you can think of a workspace as a way to abstract how a solution, projects, and files should be managed. The following code shows how you can use different implementations of the Workspace class (AdhocWorkspace and MSBuildWorkspace) to format your code:

```
Console.Out.WriteLine(Formatter.Format(code, new AdhocWorkspace()));
Console.Out.WriteLine(Formatter.Format(code, MSBuildWorkspace.Create()));
```

In both cases, the output is the same as it is for NormalizeWhitespace(). In other chapters we'll use workspaces for testing and project and solution management.

There's one other way you can specify how nodes should be formatted. It's by using the Annotation property on the Formatter class, like this:

```
Console.Out.WriteLine(
  code.WithAdditionalAnnotations(Formatter.Annotation));
```

If you print the node to the console window, it will look like the original node's output: classNewClass{}. However, the reason you'd want to do this is when you create a code fix, which we'll talk about in Chapter 2. The code fix engine will look for nodes that have this annotation, and format their content based on the rules specified by the developer in Visual Studio. In cases with a new node in a console application, adding this annotation doesn't change anything. However, when you're creating a code fix, using Formatter.Annotation is valulable because you can let other aspects of the Compiler API handle code formatting for you.

Conclusion

In this chapter, you received an introduction into the Compiler API world. You saw how you could parse code and create executables based on the syntax trees produce. You learned how you to create trees directly and produce new trees based on a tree's content. Finally, you saw how you can use annotations and formatting with syntax trees. In the next chapter, we'll use this newfound knowledge of trees to create diagnostics and code fixes to help you find and fix errors in your code.

CHAPTER 2

Writing Diagnostics

Chapter 1 provided a foundational tour of the Compiler API. In this chapter, you'll use that knowledge to build diagnostics. You'll learn how to quickly find issues in code and provide code fixes to a developer when appropriate. You'll also learn how to write unit tests for diagnostics and code fixes as well as debug your diagnostic code.

The Need to Diagnose Compilation

One of the first rules that I learned as a software developer is to "fail fast." The quicker you can find an issue in your code, the less damage it can do (especially if you find it on your machine, then no one can blame or make fun of you). Consider this example: in 1997, I was working on a very stressful project, in part because it didn't have any testing in place, and I was about to go on my honeymoon. I was one of only two developers on the project, and the rest of the project team was concerned about resolving issues while I was away. We spent a fair amount of time testing the code before I left, but unfortunately it wasn't enough. During my leave, the application didn't process data correctly as it should, and the other developers had to scramble to find the problem. When I returned, people were not happy. The problem was supposedly due to one line of code that didn't handle boolean logic correctly. The moral of this story is to slow down and introduce a strict process to ongoing development that results in a stable application with better testing. Not being able to find the existing error at all resulted in a lot of preventable tension and grief.

Now, a problem like this can't be found by tooling. Meaning, a tool doesn't know if "if(!isValid)" or "if(isValid)" is "correct" based on what the application needs to do. But there are many cases in which developers need to follow specific idioms. If they don't, really bad things can happen, like an entire service can crash. Case in point: while working on an application in 2007 that used Windows Communication Foundation (WCF), I created an operation that was one-way, which looked something like this:

```
[OperationContract(IsOneWay = true)]
public string MyOperation() { return null; }
```

J. Bock, *.NET Development Using the Compiler API*, DOI 10.1007/978-1-4842-2111-2_2

■ **Note** For more information about a one-way operation, see `https://msdn.`
`microsoft.com/en-us/library/system.servicemodel.operationcontractattribute.`
`isoneway%28v=vs.110%29.aspx.`

What the method did isn't important. What *is* important is how the operation was defined. It's marked with the `OperationContractAttribute` with `IsOneWay` set to true. This means that as soon as the service starts handling the request, the client can move on. This is nice for processing event data where the client doesn't want to wait for that processing to finish, but if you make a method one-way, you can't return anything from it. My method was returning a `string`. This is a problem that will cause an exception, but I didn't see it until I actually hosted the service and invoked it from a client. If I ran a unit test against the code where I wasn't hosting the service, it worked. Compilation was also fine—the C# compiler has no knowledge of specific idioms that frameworks must enforce. So I thought I was good...until we tried to run it in our development environment, and it failed miserably. Granted, this didn't get into production, but I didn't fail fast.

The ideal situation would've been to know there was an issue as soon as I typed that code into Visual Studio. However, in 2007, there really wasn't a way to do this. Sure, you could write a custom FxCop/Code Analysis rule to check for this issue, but you would have to wait until you compiled the code to find it. Knowing as soon as you write the code is the fastest "fail fast" you can do.

■ **Note** To learn how to make custom code analysis rules in VS2010 run in FxCop and
VS2008, see `http://blog.tatham.oddie.com.au/2010/01/06/custom-code-analysis-`
`rules-in-vs2010-and-how-to-make-them-run-in-fxcop-and-vs2008-too/.`

Now, with the Compiler API, you *can* write a diagnostic that will analyze portions of your code to see if they have any issues that the C# compiler doesn't know about. You control the rules that are enforced. Here are some examples:

- You don't want any developers using `DateTime.Now`; rather, `DateTime.UtcNow` should be used to catch any places in code where `DateTime` instances are obtained as a local kind.

- All classes that inherit from a certain base class should be serializable.

- You want to put a `TimeSpan` value into an attribute, but you can't do that directly; you have to use a string value formatted to a `TimeSpan`, so you want to verify that the value is formatted correctly.

You can probably come up with others based on your own development experiences, which is why diagnostics are such a powerful feature in the new compiler and its integration into Visual Studio. Most rules, idioms, practices, and so on can be codified into a diagnostic that will run for everyone on the development team so issues can be identified and (potentially) automatically fixed. In the next section, we'll examine the details of creating a diagnostic with a code fix.

Designing the Diagnostic

Having the desire to find issues in code is one thing. But how do you do it? Let's spend a bit of time going over the design process first and how you can use the Syntax Visualizer to assist your diagnostic implementation.

Understanding the Problem

As you saw in Chapter 1, the Compiler API is vast, and it's easy to get lost. Knowing exactly what the problem is and all the potential variants that can crop up in code can be overwhelming, depending on the nature of the issue you're trying to find. No matter how well-designed the Compiler API is, we're still dealing with tokens, parsing and semantics, so we need to have a good understanding of what we're trying to find in code.

Let's go through an example of enforcing a particular coding standard. In my experience I've sometimes seen frameworks expose classes that defined virtual methods that had to be invoked if the method was overriden. For example, a base class may look something like this:

```
public class MyBaseClass
{
  protected virtual void OnInitialize() { /* ... */ }
}
```

If you inherited from this class, you needed to do this:

```
public class MySubClass
  : MyBaseClass
{
  protected override void OnInitialize()
  {
    base.OnInitialize();
    /* ... */
  }
}
```

In other words, you had to call the base class's implementation, and then you could add in whatever implementation you needed to do.

The problem with this approach is that there's no way to enforce it with the C# compiler. Overridden methods are not required to call the "base" implementation, yet with some designs this is a requirement. Unfortunately, you could easily override OnInitialize() and forget to call the base class's implementation and the C# compiler will happily produce an assembly based on your errant code. Adding XML documentation to the method helps, but it doesn't *enforce* that requirement, and that's what we really need.

So, let's write a diagnostic that checks if the base class's implementation is invoked somewhere within our overridden implementation. We'll only concern ourselves with virtual methods that are marked with a MustInvokeAttribute. If a subclass overrides that method, it must call the base class's implementation. That sounds like a good plan, but what are we going to need to look for in a syntax tree to handle this analysis correctly? In the next section, we'll use the Syntax Visualizer to get a clearer picture of the possibilities.

Using the Syntax Visualizer

Getting a vision for what an analyzer will need to do from a design perspective is a good thing, but we'll need more information. Specifically, we have to dig into a syntax tree to find the nodes to see what it is we're really looking for—for example, we'll need to find the nodes related to method calls and whether or not they're virtual. Figure 2-1 shows the tree for the code you saw in the "Understanding the Problem" section.

```
▲ MethodDeclaration [2225..2312)
    ▷ ProtectedKeyword [2225..2234)
    ▷ OverrideKeyword [2235..2243)
    ▷ PredefinedType [2244..2248)
       IdentifierToken [2249..2261)
    ▷ ParameterList [2261..2263)
    ▲ Block [2267..2312)
       ▷ OpenBraceToken [2267..2268)
       ▲ ExpressionStatement [2273..2293)
          ▲ InvocationExpression [2273..2292)
             ▲ SimpleMemberAccessExpression [2273..2290)
                ▷ BaseExpression [2273..2277)
                   DotToken [2277..2278)
                ▲ IdentifierName [2278..2290)
                   IdentifierToken [2278..2290)
```

Figure 2-1. *Discovering which nodes are in play for method invocations*

To get this screenshot, I highlighted the "OnInitialize" base method call in the overriden method. That's why the IdentifierNameSyntax node is highlighted. It's a child of an InvocationExpressionSyntax node, which in turn is a child of a MethodDeclaration.

That tells us about the definition of a method and its structure, but we want to find out that if a method is an override, and the method it's overriding has [MustInvoke], then we have to find at least one invocation of that base class method in the method's definition.

We'll attack the problem from two angles. If the user is adding a method invocation in code, we'll keep looking at the parent nodes until we either get a null or a MethodDeclarationSyntax reference. If the user is declaring or changing a method declaration, we want to examine that "root" node for child invocations. Either way, once we get a MethodDeclarationSyntax reference, we'll check to see if it's overriding a method that is marked with [MustInvoke]. If it is, then we'll look through all of its descendants for InvocationExpressionSyntax nodes and determine if at least one of those invocations is the base method. If we don't find any, then we'll report that as a diagnostic issue. To implement this approach, we'll need to work with both syntax nodes and objects that come from a semantic model, as you'll see in the next section.

By the way, where is this MustInvokeAttribute class defined? I put it into a separate assembly called MustInvokeBaseMethod. It's a good idea to separate the analyzer from the rest of your main code that you'll be analyzing. Even though in this case we have an assembly with only one attribute, we still want that diagnostic code out of what would normally be an assembly that has all of our logic and structure in it.

In the next section, we'll finally get into the details of a diagnostic.

Creating a Diagnostic

We now have a fairly good idea of what we need to look for in code for this diagnostic, which we'll call MustInvokeBaseMethodAnalyzer. In this section, you'll learn how to get the right projects and classes in place to build the diagnostic.

Using the Template

In the "Visualizing Trees" section in Chapter 1, we walked through a couple of installation steps to get the Syntax Visualizer in place. This also installed a couple of templates to make it easier to create diagnostics and refactorings. Let's use them to get our projects in place.

Create a solution in Visual Studio, and add a new project to that solution (File ➤ New ➤ Project, or Ctrl+Shift+N). You should see an option under the Extensibility node called Analyzer with Code Fix (NuGet + VSIX) as shown in Figure 2-2.

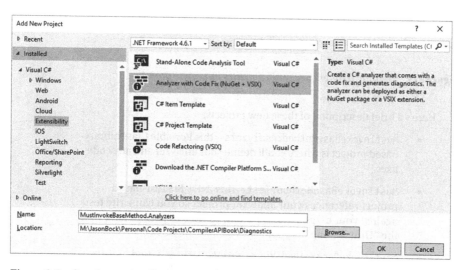

Figure 2-2. *Creating a new diagnostic project*

The resulting solution will have three new projects in it, as Figure 2-3 shows.

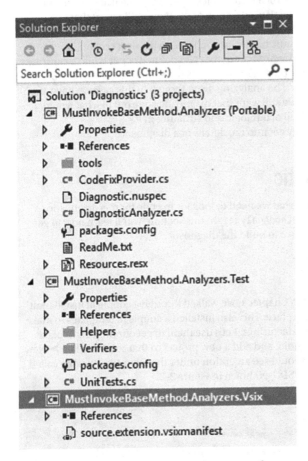

Figure 2-3. *Creating a diagnostic project creates three new projects*

Here's a brief description of these new projects:

- `MustInvokeBaseMethod.Analyzers`—this Portable Class Library-based project is where you'll define your analyzer and any code fixes.

- `MustInvokeBaseMethod.Test`—this .NET MSTest-based project references your analyzer project so you can write tests against your diagnostic. We'll talk about this project later in the "Unit Testing" section.

- `MustInvokeBaseMethod.Vsix`—this VS Package-based project references your analyzer and allows you to quickly test your analyzer code in a new Visual Studio instance.

When you create a diagnostic project, the template will generate a diagnostic that looks for types with lowercase letters and provides a code fix to make the name all uppercase. It's kind of a silly rule, but it does illustrate the machinery you need in place to ensure your diagnostic is implemented correctly. In the next section, we'll build the diagnostic and code fix for our base virtual method scenario, but if you've never built one before, I encourage you to take a look at that code just to see how it's laid out.

■ **Note**   I personally don't like the layout of the projects. If you get the source code, you'll notice the directory structure is slightly different than what the template generates, and I've also deleted a fair amount of boilerplate code that it generates. Keep in mind that the template is a good start, but as your experience with diagnostics increases, you'll probably want to change the code as well. Also, you don't have to use the template. Maybe you don't want the VSIX project, or you want to use a different testing framework than MSTest. Feel free to experiment as you become more familiar with diagnostics and how they work.

One other project that we'll add is the MustInvokeBaseMethod project. All this will contain is the MustInvokeAttribute—its definition looks like this:

```
[AttributeUsage(AttributeTargets.Method,
  AllowMultiple = false, Inherited = true)]
public sealed class MustInvokeAttribute
  : Attribute
{ }
```

This may seem like a bit of overkill, having a project to contain just one type, but it's best to separate your analyzer code from the code you're going to analyze. Remember, the analyzer project is a Portable Class Library (PCL), and it can't reference assemblies that are not PCLs, so if you put all your code into the same assembly, this would force your main code to follow the same PCL restrictions. PCLs have a limited set of APIs that they can use from the .NET Framework, and, depending on what your code needs to do, you may end up not being able to implement certain features. Also, keep in mind that when you keep code separated in a non-PCL project, the analyzer project can't reference that MustInvokeBaseMethod project, but that's okay. Keeping a strict boundary between the analyzer and the code to analyze also removes issues like versioning, and most of the time you'll discover nodes via their names, not by a specific type.

Building the Diagnostic

We've covered the basics of the diagnostic design and how to use the analyzer project template. Let's get into the details of how you set up and implement a diagnostic.

Diagnostic Class Setup

The first thing that needs to be done is get the class definition correct. Here's the definition of the analyzer, which was lifted from the analyzer generated from the project template:

```
[DiagnosticAnalyzer(LanguageNames.CSharp)]
public sealed class MustInvokeBaseMethodAnalyzer
  : DiagnosticAnalyzer
{
  /* ... */
}
```

Note that you add the DiagnosticAnalyzer attribute to the class definition as well as use DiagnosticAnalyzer as the base class. Using DiagnosticAnalyzer in the inheritance hierarchy requires you to implement two virtual members that you'll see in a moment. The attribute is used primarily by tools like Visual Studio that will use its existence to discover the class and use it as an analyzer. Although we don't talk about VB in this book, you can write analyzers for VB just as easily as you can for C#. In fact, if your analyzer is generic enough, it's possible to write an analyzer in one language that can target both languages.

When you inherit from DiagnosticAnalyzer, you have to override two abstract members: a read-only SupportedDiagnostics property and an Initialize() method. Listing 2-1 shows how they are defined.

Listing 2-1. Defining required diagnostic members

```
private static DiagnosticDescriptor rule = new DiagnosticDescriptor(
  "MUST0001", "Find Overridden Methods That do Not Call the Base Class's
  Method",
  "Virtual methods with [MustInvoke] must be invoked in overrides",
  "Usage", DiagnosticSeverity.Error, true);

public override ImmutableArray<DiagnosticDescriptor> SupportedDiagnostics
{
  get
  {
    return ImmutableArray.Create(
      MustInvokeBaseMethodAnalyzer.rule);
  }
}

public override void Initialize(AnalysisContext context)
{
  context.RegisterSyntaxNodeAction<SyntaxKind>(
    this.AnalyzeMethodDeclaration, SyntaxKind.MethodDeclaration);
}
```

An analyzer can support multiple diagnostics. This means that you can report on more that one issue from an analyzer. In our case, there's only one scenario we need to find, so we'll only return one DiagnosticDescriptor rule within an ImmutableArray. The ImmutableArray class comes from the System.Collections.Immutable assembly, which you can use from any .NET project because it's in NuGet.

A DiagnosticDescriptor object defines a number of characteristics about an analyzer violation. Some of these constructor values are descriptions that will be used to help you understand why code is being shown with an issue. The first value is an identifier, which you use to relate specific rule violations to code fixes—you'll see this put to use later in the "Providing Code Fixes" section. You can also specify the severity of the violation with the DiagnosticSeverity enumeration. An Error value will show up as a red squiggle under the bad code in Visual Studio, whereas a Warning level creates a yellow squiggle. Finally, the isEnabledByDefault argument value specifies that the analyzer should be enabled as soon as Visual Studio finds it.

The Initialize() method is used to inform the Compiler API engine of the specific nodes you want to analyze. In our example, we want to focus on MethodDefinitionSyntax nodes, so we used RegisterSyntaxNodeAction(). The first argument is an Action<SyntaxNodeAnalysisContext>, which is where we'll figure out if a method has virtual method issues. We'll cover what AnalyzeMethodDeclaration() does in the next section, "Analyzing Code." There are other "Register" methods on the context object that you can use to handle other actions, like RegisterSymbolAction() and RegisterCompilationAction(). You may want to use these methods to handle different parts and phases of the compilation process. As always, experiment and peruse the APIs—you never know when a different method may solve a problem you have in a better way.

Now that the essentials of the analyzer are in place, let's see how we determine if we have an error in our code.

Analyzing Code

Our AnalyzeMethodDeclaration() method is where we need to figure out if a virtual base method must be invoked. The method is somewhat long, so we'll go over it in two pieces. Listing 2-2 contains the first part.

Listing 2-2. Starting the implementation of the diagnostic's analysis.

```
private void AnalyzeMethodDeclaration(SyntaxNodeAnalysisContext context)
{
  var method = context.Node as MethodDeclarationSyntax;
  var model = context.SemanticModel;
  var methodSymbol = model.GetDeclaredSymbol(method) as IMethodSymbol;
```

```
context.CancellationToken.ThrowIfCancellationRequested();

if(methodSymbol.IsOverride)
{
    var overriddenMethod = methodSymbol.OverriddenMethod;

    var hasAttribute = false;
    foreach (var attribute in overriddenMethod.GetAttributes())
    {
        if(attribute.AttributeClass.Name == "MustInvokeAttribute")
        {
            hasAttribute = true;
            break;
        }
    }
}
```

The first thing we'll do is grab the MethodDeclarationSyntax node that either the user is currently working on, or a node that has been parsed. We can safely make the type cast as we said we only want nodes where the SyntaxKind is MethodDeclaration in Initialize(). Next, we'll obtain the IMethodSymbol for that node with the semantic model's GetDeclaredSyntax(), which we'll use to determine some aspects of the method. But notice that the next action is to call ThrowIfCancellationRequested() on the CancellationToken from the context. Visual Studio wants the developer to have a responsive experience, so if your analysis is going to take too long, you should exit and not report any issues. That call from the token will get you out of your analysis method quickly if a cancellation has been requested. How often you should call this method is up to you, but if your analysis method is more than a couple of lines of code, you should probably call it at least once.

Now that we have our method symbol, we want to see if it's a method that's overriding another method, which is what the IsOverride property gives us. If the method is an override, we can find the method that it's overriding via OverriddenMethod. We have to check if that overriden method has a MustInvokeAttribute on it, so we iterate through the AttributeData objects in the array returned from GetAttributes(). If at least one object has the name "MustInvokeAttribute." then we know we need to keep going further. For our example, this simple name test is sufficient. You may want to make sure that a type is within a namespace and/or within a specific assembly. In those cases, you can use the ContainingNamespace and ContainingAssembly properties to get that name information and compare these property values to expected name values.

At this point, we know we have a method that's overriden a method with [MustInvoke]. We now need to find an invocation of that base class method, otherwise we have to report an error. Listing 2-3 has the other half of AnalyzerMethodDeclaration().

Listing 2-3. Finishing the implementation of the analyzer.

```
context.CancellationToken.ThrowIfCancellationRequested();
if(hasAttribute)
{
  var invocations = method.DescendantNodes(_ => true)
    .OfType<InvocationExpressionSyntax>();
  foreach (var invocation in invocations)
  {
    var invocationSymbol = model.GetSymbolInfo(
      invocation.Expression).Symbol as IMethodSymbol;

    if (invocationSymbol == overriddenMethod)
    {
      return;
    }
  }

  context.ReportDiagnostic(Diagnostic.Create(
    MustInvokeBaseMethodAnalyzer.rule,
    method.Identifier.GetLocation()));
  }
 }
}
```

We use `DesendantNodes()` to find `InvocationExpressionSyntax` nodes. If one of them is the same as the overriden method, we're good. We use `GetSymbolInfo()` to obtain an `IMethodSymbol` reference based on the invocation's `Expression` property. If that reference equals the overriden method, we're done.

If we don't find a call to the base class method, we report an error via `ReportDiagnostic()`. We use `GetLocation()` on the identifier from the original `MethodDeclarationSyntax` node. This means that Visual Studio will add a red squiggle under the method definition's name. If we used `GetLocation()` off of the `MethodDefinitionSyntax` node itself, the squiggle would be under the entire method. It's somewhat of an aesthetic choice. Lots of red will get a developer's attention, but it may also be too broad of a UI hint, especially if the method is large. Again, use what you think best serves the developer who uses your analyzer.

With the analyzer in place, we can think about writing a code fix to provide an automatic way to correct the error for the developer. We'll do that next.

Providing Code Fixes

It's great that we can alert a developer of an issue as soon as they make it; what would make it better is fixing it for them as well. You can write code fixes for analyzers that do just that. Before we look at the code that does this, let's think about how we can create a fix for [`MustInvoke`].

Designing the Fix

Let's start by looking at a couple of coding conditions that can happen in a method. If our base method looks like this:

```
protected virtual void OnInitialize()
```

It's pretty easy to create a fix—all we need to do is call it like this:

```
base.OnInitilize();
```

Therefore, we just need to generate an invocation. But there's far more you can do with a method. What if the method is defined like this?

```
unsafe protected virtual int[] OnInitialize(string a, Guid b, char* c, ref
long d);
```

Now we have a return value, arguments that take pointer types and a ref argument as well. Fixing it would take code that looks like this:

```
var onInitializeResult = base.OnInitialize(a, b, c, ref d);
```

Fortunately, we can just pass in the parameters from the overriden method to this method invocation. The developer may want to change that, but a code fix can do this as a simplistic heuristic and let the developer choose to alter it as needed. The developer can also ignore the code fix entirely and correct the issue manually. Providing a code fix does not require the developer to use it; it's just another way to assist the developer.

Of course, we're assuming that there isn't a variable called onInitializeResult. We'll need to make sure that we check all local variables and see if there are any that have that name. If so, we'll have to come up with some heuristic to ensure the name is unique without coming up with an ugly name with random characters. Writing a good code fix means you try to generate code that a developer would accept as their own.

So, here's what we need to do with this code fix:

- Determine if there are any arguments for the method invocation. If so, use the current method definition's parameters.

- Determine if there's a return value. If so, we'll capture that with a simple "var" statement, generating a variable name that is unique.

- We'll also make sure that our added invocation is the first statement that occurs in the overridden method.

Now that we have a plan in place, let's implement the code fix.

Implementing the Fix

First, here's the definition of the code fix class:

```
[ExportCodeFixProvider(LanguageNames.CSharp)]
[Shared]
public sealed class MustInvokeBaseMethodCallMethodCodeFix
  : CodeFixProvider
{
  /* ... */
}
```

You need to add the ExportCodeFixProvider and Shared attributes as well as inherit from the CodeFixProvider class for your code fix to work correctly. When you inherit from CodeFixProvider, there are two members that you must provide implementations for: the FixableDiagnosticIds property and the RegisterCodeFixesAsync method. The property is easy to implement:

```
public override ImmutableArray<string> FixableDiagnosticIds
{
  get
  {
    return ImmutableArray.Create("MUST0001");
  }
}
```

The identifier we pass into the array is the same one that the diagnostic uses for the rule it reports when a code violation is detected. This is used to tie the rule and fix together so Visual Studio can provide the fix for the issue.

Before we get to RegisterCodeFixesAsync() (in the next section), there's another virtual member that you don't have to override, but you should: GetFixAllProvider():

```
public override FixAllProvider GetFixAllProvider()
{
  return WellKnownFixAllProviders.BatchFixer;
}
```

This tells Visual Studio that if there are other occurrences of this code issue within a selected scope (document, project, or solution), Visual Studio will automatically apply the fix within that scope. The default implementation for this method in CodeFixProvider is to return null, so if you want Visual Studio to do fixes for you solution-wide, you should have the method return BatchFixer.

■ **Note**   If you want see how CodeFixProvider is implemented, visit this link:
`http://source.roslyn.io/#Microsoft.CodeAnalysis.Workspaces/CodeFixes/`
`CodeFixProvider.cs`.

Now that the boilerplate is out of the way, let's add this fix. We're going to do it two ways: one that generates trees and the other that parses a statement in a string. Let's do the tree approach first.

Using Syntax Trees

Here's the implementation for creating a base method invocation. We'll start with the general implementation of `RegisterCodeFixesAsync()`, which is shown in Listing 2-4.

Listing 2-4. Implementing RegisterCodeFixesAsync() in a Code Fix class.

```
public override async Task RegisterCodeFixesAsync(CodeFixContext context)
{
  var root = await context.Document.GetSyntaxRootAsync(
    context.CancellationToken).ConfigureAwait(false);

  context.CancellationToken.ThrowIfCancellationRequested();

  var diagnostic = context.Diagnostics[0];
  var methodNode = root.FindNode(diagnostic.Location.SourceSpan) as
  MethodDeclarationSyntax;

  var model = await context.Document.GetSemanticModelAsync(
    context.CancellationToken);
  var methodSymbol = model.GetDeclaredSymbol(methodNode) as IMethodSymbol;

  var invocation = MustInvokeBaseMethodCallMethodCodeFix.CreateInvocation(
    methodSymbol);
  invocation = MustInvokeBaseMethodCallMethodCodeFix.AddArguments(
    context, methodSymbol, invocation);
  var statement = MustInvokeBaseMethodCallMethodCodeFix.CreateStatement(
    context, methodNode, methodSymbol, invocation);
  var newRoot = MustInvokeBaseMethodCallMethodCodeFix.CreateNewRoot(
    root, methodNode, statement);

  const string codeFixDescription = "Add base invocation";
  context.RegisterCodeFix(
    CodeAction.Create(codeFixDescription,
    _ => Task.FromResult(context.Document.WithSyntaxRoot(newRoot)),
    codeFixDescription), diagnostic);
}
```

The first thing we do is get the `MethodDeclarationSyntax` node for the method that had the issue in the first place. We get its location from the `Diagnostics` array property and then find it from the `SyntaxNode` tree node. Then we pull its related `IMethodSymbol` from the semantic model, which will make our lives a little easier later on.

Now we build our `InvocationExpressionSyntax` node in `CreateInvocation()`:

```
private static InvocationExpressionSyntax CreateInvocation(
  IMethodSymbol methodSymbol)
{
  return SyntaxFactory.InvocationExpression(
    SyntaxFactory.MemberAccessExpression(
        SyntaxKind.SimpleMemberAccessExpression,
      SyntaxFactory.BaseExpression().WithToken(
        SyntaxFactory.Token(SyntaxKind.BaseKeyword)),
        SyntaxFactory.IdentifierName(
          methodSymbol.Name))
    .WithOperatorToken(
        SyntaxFactory.Token(
          SyntaxKind.DotToken)));
}
```

This code generates an expression like this: "base.BaseMethod()". Calling `BaseExpression()` provides the "base" keyword, and `IdentifierName()` creates the name of the method to invoke.

Next, we have to add any arguments to the invocation if needed—this is shown in Listing 2-5.

Listing 2-5. Adding arguments for the base method invocation.

```
private static InvocationExpressionSyntax AddArguments(
  CodeFixContext context, IMethodSymbol methodSymbol,
  InvocationExpressionSyntax invocation)
{
  context.CancellationToken.ThrowIfCancellationRequested();

  var argumentCount = methodSymbol.Parameters.Length;
  if (argumentCount > 0)
  {
    // Define an argument list.
    var arguments = new SyntaxNodeOrToken[(2 * argumentCount) - 1];

    for (var i = 0; i < argumentCount; i++)
    {
      var parameter = methodSymbol.Parameters[i];
      var argument = SyntaxFactory.Argument(
        SyntaxFactory.IdentifierName(parameter.Name));
```

```
if (parameter.RefKind.HasFlag(RefKind.Ref))
{
  argument = argument.WithRefOrOutKeyword(
    SyntaxFactory.Token(SyntaxKind.RefKeyword));
}
else if (parameter.RefKind.HasFlag(RefKind.Out))
{
  argument = argument.WithRefOrOutKeyword(
    SyntaxFactory.Token(SyntaxKind.OutKeyword));
}

arguments[2 * i] = argument;

if (i < argumentCount - 1)
{
  arguments[(2 * i) + 1] = SyntaxFactory.Token(SyntaxKind.CommaToken);
}
}

invocation = invocation.WithArgumentList(
  SyntaxFactory.ArgumentList(
    SyntaxFactory.SeparatedList<ArgumentSyntax>(arguments))
  .WithOpenParenToken(SyntaxFactory.Token(SyntaxKind.OpenParenToken))
  .WithCloseParenToken(SyntaxFactory.Token(SyntaxKind.CloseParenToken)));
}

return invocation;
}
```

If arguments are necessary, we build up the argument list via `SyntaxFactory.Argument()`. If the parameter is a `ref` or an `out`, we add those keywords with `WithRefOrOutKeyword`. We also have to separate each argument with a `SyntaxToken` of kind `SyntaxKind.CommaToken`. That's why the arguments array's size looks a little awkward at first. For example, if we have four arguments, we need to generate four `ArgumentSyntax` objects plus three `SyntaxToken` representing the commas between the arguments, which means the array will have seven elements. Once we have all of the arguments, we add them to invocation via `WithArgumentList()`, remembering to reassign invocation to the return value.

Now we need to create a `StatementSyntax` node that will contain the invocation. This is where we'll handle the call if it returns a value or not, which is showing in Listing 2-6.

Listing 2-6. Creating a statement for the method invocation

```
private static StatementSyntax CreateStatement(CodeFixContext context,
  MethodDeclarationSyntax methodNode, IMethodSymbol methodSymbol,
  InvocationExpressionSyntax invocation)
{
  context.CancellationToken.ThrowIfCancellationRequested();

  StatementSyntax statement = null;

  if (!methodSymbol.ReturnsVoid)
  {
    var returnValueSafeName = CreateSafeLocalVariableName(
      methodNode, methodSymbol);

    statement = SyntaxFactory.LocalDeclarationStatement(
      SyntaxFactory.VariableDeclaration(
        SyntaxFactory.IdentifierName("var"))

      .WithVariables(SyntaxFactory.SingletonSeparatedList
        <VariableDeclaratorSyntax>(
        SyntaxFactory.VariableDeclarator(
          SyntaxFactory.Identifier(returnValueSafeName))
        .WithInitializer(SyntaxFactory.EqualsValueClause(invocation)))));
  }
  else
  {
    statement = SyntaxFactory.ExpressionStatement(invocation);
  }

  return statement.WithAdditionalAnnotations(Formatter.Annotation);
}
```

If we have to handle a return value, we create a local variable and assign the return value to that. We get the name of this local variable from CreateSafeLocalVariable Name() - Listing 2-7 shows what it looks like.

Listing 2-7. Creating a safe variable name for a return value

```
private static string CreateSafeLocalVariableName(
  MethodDeclarationSyntax methodNode, IMethodSymbol methodSymbol)
{
  var localDeclarations = methodNode.DescendantNodes(
    _ => true).OfType<VariableDeclaratorSyntax>();
  var returnValueName =
    $"{methodSymbol.Name.Substring(0, 1).ToLower()}{methodSymbol.Name.
    Substring(1)}Result";
  var returnValueSafeName = returnValueName;
  var returnValueCount = 0;
```

```
while (localDeclarations.Any(_ =>
  _.Identifier.Text == returnValueSafeName))
{
  returnValueSafeName = $"{returnValueName}{returnValueCount}";
  returnValueCount++;
}

return returnValueSafeName;
}
```

We use the name of the method as a base for the variable name (making it camel-cased in the process), and keep adding a numeric value to the end until we find a unique name. The chances of us even getting into the while loop once is extremely small, but with this code in place we don't ever have to worry about running into a collision.

Finally, once the statement is generated, we register a code fix on the context via RegisterCodeFix(), which uses a new root created from CreateNewRoot():

```
private static SyntaxNode CreateNewRoot(
  SyntaxNode root, MethodDeclarationSyntax methodNode,
  StatementSyntax statement)
{
  var body = methodNode.Body;
  var firstNode = body.ChildNodes().FirstOrDefault();

  var newBody = firstNode != null ?
    body.InsertNodesBefore(body.ChildNodes().First(),
      new[] { statement }) :
    SyntaxFactory.Block(statement);

  var newRoot = root.ReplaceNode(body, newBody);
  return newRoot;
}
```

Notice that we have to be a bit careful in the case in which the method doesn't have any code in it. In that case, the body won't have any child nodes, so we can just create a new BlockSyntax node. Otherwise, we insert our new StatementSyntax node as the first child node in the method's body.

Parsing Statements

Although creating trees like the ones you saw in the previous section aren't too hard, it's also not an easy endeavor. I had to use a combination of the Syntax Visualizer and RoslynQuoter tools to ensure I was generating the right nodes. This is kind of tedious. Fortunately, there's an alternative approach that you can use in some scenarios that results in a lot less code than creating trees and nodes manually. You can generate the code you want as a string, and then use SyntaxFactory's ParseStatement() to give you a StatementSyntax node directly. Listing 2-8 shows how that's done.

Listing 2-8. Using ParseStatement() to generate a tree

```
private static StatementSyntax CreateStatement(
  MethodDeclarationSyntax methodNode, IMethodSymbol methodSymbol)
{
  var methodParameters = methodSymbol.Parameters;
  var arguments = new string[methodParameters.Length];

  for(var i = 0; i < methodParameters.Length; i++)
  {
    var parameter = methodParameters[i];
    var argument = parameter.Name;

    if (parameter.RefKind.HasFlag(RefKind.Ref))
    {
      argument = $"ref {argument}";
    }
    else if (parameter.RefKind.HasFlag(RefKind.Out))
    {
      argument = $"out {argument}";
    }

    arguments[i] = argument;
  }

  var methodCall =
    $"base.{methodSymbol.Name}({string.Join(", ", arguments)});
    {Environment.NewLine}";

  if(!methodSymbol.ReturnsVoid)
  {
    var variableName = MustInvokeBaseMethodCallMethodCodeFix.
    CreateSafeLocalVariableName(
      methodNode, methodSymbol);
    methodCall = $"var {variableName} = {methodCall}";
  }

  return SyntaxFactory.ParseStatement(methodCall)
    .WithAdditionalAnnotations(Formatter.Annotation);
}
```

Logically, this code ends up at the same spots as the other approach but with a lot less code. Essentially, a statement is created, like "var onInitializeResult = base. OnInitialize(a, b);", and then this string is passed into ParseStatement(). That's it! Note that there are other "Parse" methods on SyntaxFactory, like ParseExpression() and ParseArgumentList(). Depending on the kind of code fix you need to make, it may be easier to generate the code in a string and let SyntaxFactory do the heavy lifting.

■ **Note** You may be wondering which technique you should use: tree generation or text parsing. This article does a great job analyzing each option, providing suggestions when you should use one over the other: `http://blog.comealive.io/Syntax-Factory-Vs-Parse-Text/`.

Executing the Diagnostic and Code Fix

After all that work, it's finally time to see our code run in Visual Studio. The easiest way to do this is to make the VSIX project the startup solution and run that project. It'll create a new instance of Visual Studio with the analyzer installed as an extension (we'll talk more about deployments in the "Deploying and Installing Diagnostics" section). Create a new solution, and create a base class with a virtual method that has the [MustInvoke] on it.

■ **Note** Because we're only looking for an attribute by name and we don't look at the name of its containing assembly, you could create an attribute in this test project with the name "MustInvokeAttribute". You could also reference the project and/or its resultant assembly that we created before that has the attribute already defined.

Create a class that inherits from the base class, override the virtual method, but don't call it. You should see a red squiggle under the method definition, as Figure 2-4 shows.

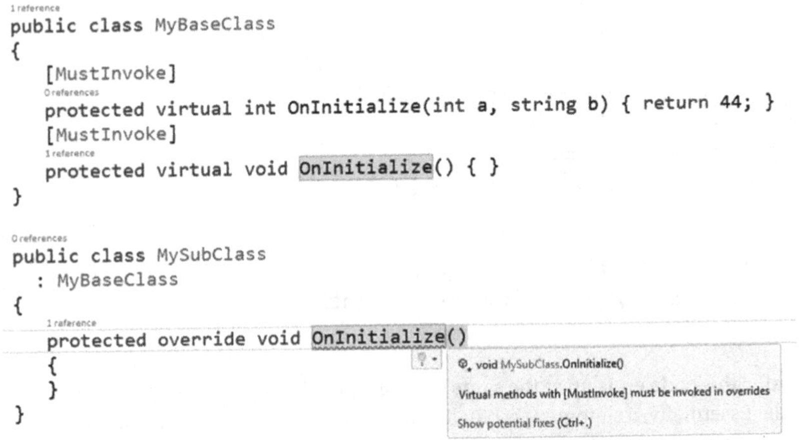

```
1 reference
public class MyBaseClass
{
    [MustInvoke]
    0 references
    protected virtual int OnInitialize(int a, string b) { return 44; }
    [MustInvoke]
    1 reference
    protected virtual void OnInitialize() { }
}

0 references
public class MySubClass
    : MyBaseClass
{
    1 reference
    protected override void OnInitialize()
    {
    }
}
```

Ⓧ, void MySubClass.OnInitialize()

Virtual methods with [MustInvoke] must be invoked in overrides

Show potential fixes (Ctrl+.)

***Figure 2-4.** Getting the diagnostic to display in Visual Studio*

Now, move the cursor so it's on the method definition, and press Ctrl + ".". You should see the code fix window pop up with a code diff view, as shown in Figure 2-5.

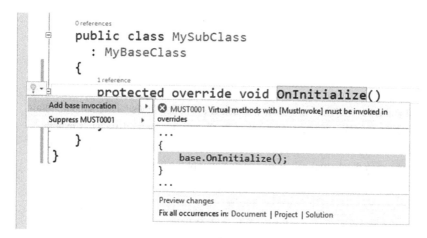

Figure 2-5. *Getting the code fix to display in Visual Studio*

Notice the options at the bottom of the popup. If there were other base method invocation issues like this in the document, project, or solution, we could choose to fix them all at once. Applying the fix makes the error go away!

We can also make the method take some arguments and return a value—the code fix handles it as expected. If we had this code in place:

```
protected override int OnInitialize(int a, string b)
{
  return 43;
}
```

Figure 2-6 shows what the code fix would do.

```
2 references
protected override int OnInitialize(int a, string b)
{
    var onInitializeResult = base.OnInitialize(a, b);
    return 43;
}
```

Figure 2-6. *Calling the base method with a return value*

If we had a variable that collided with our initial choice, Figure 2-7 shows that we won't collide with it.

```
2 references
protected override int OnInitialize(int a, string b)
{|
    var onInitializeResult0 = base.OnInitialize(a, b);
    var onInitializeResult = 43 + a;
    return onInitializeResult;
}
```

Figure 2-7. *Generating a local variable with a unique name*

■ **Note**   If you type "override" in a class and select the option in Visual Studio to generate the override, it'll automatically generate a call to the base class method, which is exactly what we want. But the reason this diagnostic and code fix is in place is to guard against developers who may delete that call when the designer of the base class requires the invocation.

Diagnostics and code fixes are formidable tools to have, and they're not as complex as they may seem at first glance. The core of this diagnostic is only 40 lines of code, while the code fix (using the parsing technique) is under 50 lines of code. The key is to figure out what you're targeting in your code and the possible cases you can run into.

Having the ability to write diagnostics is powerful because you're able to enforce coding standards and desired idioms along with providing automatic code fixes, but you're still dealing with parsing, trees, and so on. It's crucial to have good testing in place to ensure that your code works as expected. That's what we'll cover in the next section.

Debugging Diagnostics

You've seen how diagnostics and code fixes can reduce the amount of bugs in a code base and enforce framework standards and expectations. In this section, we'll cover how you can test and diagnose issues with your analyzers.

Unit Testing

When I am consulting at a client, one factor that I use to determine the health of a project is this: are there a large suite of unit tests that developers can run quickly? This isn't a guarantee that the project is stable, but it's definitely a key aspect. Given how complex compiler code can get, it's important to have those tests in place.

When you create the diagnostic project, the template creates an MSTest-based class library with some helper code to assist you with writing tests that target analyzers and code fixes. Over time I've created my own set of helper methods, which is included in the code for this book. As you get more familiar with the Compiler API you'll probably add your own as well. You may choose to delete the project and create your own test project using a different testing framework like NUnit, xUnit or Fixie. Whatever you choose to do, I strongly encourage you to write tests, especially if you end up changing your implementation. Even if you don't change your code after you've written it once, write the tests!

Let's begin by looking at some tests you could write for the analyzer. In the first scenario, the test will check to ensure the analyzer doesn't fire if a base method has [MustInvoke] but the overriden method calls the base method. In the second scenario, the text should fire the analyzer as the overriden method does not invoke the base method. There are other cases to cover (and they're in the source code) but we'll just cover these two in the book. Here's the first scenario:

```
[TestMethod]
[Case("Case2")]
public async Task Case2Test()
{
    await TestHelpers.RunAnalysisAsync<MustInvokeBaseMethodAnalyzer>(
        $@"Targets\{nameof(MustInvokeBaseMethodAnalyzerTests)}\Case2.cs",
        new string[0]);
}
```

The TestHelpers class contains a number of methods that I use to make analyzer and code fix tests easier to write. I'll show you what RunAnalysisAsync() does in a moment, but first let's address some other aspects of the test.

The actual name of the test method is longer in the code, so I shortened it for the book. The CaseAttribute is just a way to mark which case is being tested. As you can see in the partial file path, that name is used to put test code in separate folders so they can be loaded in the right test. Here's what Case2.cs looks like:

```
using MustInvokeBaseMethod;

namespace
  MustInvokeBaseMethod.Analyzers.Test.Targets.
  MustInvokeBaseMethodAnalyzerTests
{
  public class Case2Base
  {
    [MustInvoke]
    public virtual void Method() { }
  }

  public class Case2Sub
    : Case3Base
  {
    public override void Method()
    {
      base.Method();
    }
  }
}
```

The Build Action property for this file in Visual Studio is set to "None", and the Copy to Output Directory value is set to "Copy always". This way, you can use the Syntax Visualizer in Visual Studio to see the structure of your code and find the location of the span where a diagnostic will report an error without having the code compiled as part of your test assembly. Plus, by copying it to the output directory you can load its textual context and give it to an analyzer. Let's now take a look at RunAnalysisAsync() to see how all of the test code ties together—this is in Listing 2-9.

Listing 2-9. Testing diagnostics against source code.

```
internal static async Task RunAnalysisAsync<T>(string path,
    string[] diagnosticIds,
    Action<ImmutableArray<Diagnostic>> diagnosticInspector = null)
    where T : DiagnosticAnalyzer, new()
{
    var code = File.ReadAllText(path);
    var diagnostics = await TestHelpers.GetDiagnosticsAsync(
        code, new T());
    Assert.AreEqual(diagnosticIds.Length, diagnostics.Count(),
        nameof(Enumerable.Count));

    foreach (var diagnosticId in diagnosticIds)
    {
        Assert.IsTrue(diagnostics.Any(_ => _.Id == diagnosticId),
            diagnosticId);
    }

    diagnosticInspector?.Invoke(diagnostics);
}
```

RunAnalysisAsync() loads the code in the given file with ReadAllText(). Then it passes that code into another helper method, GetDiagnosticsAsync(), along with a new instance of the diagnostic whose type was specified with the T generic parameter. The following code shows you what that method does:

```
internal static async Task<ImmutableArray<Diagnostic>> GetDiagnosticsAsync(
    string code, DiagnosticAnalyzer analyzer)
{
    var document = TestHelpers.Create(code);
    var compilation = (await document.Project.GetCompilationAsync())
        .WithAnalyzers(ImmutableArray.Create(analyzer));
    return await compilation.GetAnalyzerDiagnosticsAsync();
}
```

Via Create() we're able to get a Document instance. From that, we can compile the project associated with the document, giving it the analyzer we created in RunAnalysisAsync(). Once that's done, we return the set of diagnostics back to the call. Listing 2-10 shows what Create() does.

Listing 2-10. Creating a document for test code

```
internal static Document Create(string code)
{
  var projectName = "Test";
  var projectId = ProjectId.CreateNewId(projectName);

  var solution = new AdhocWorkspace()
    .CurrentSolution
    .AddProject(projectId, projectName, projectName,
        LanguageNames.CSharp)
    .WithProjectCompilationOptions(projectId,
      new CSharpCompilationOptions(OutputKind.DynamicallyLinkedLibrary))
    .AddMetadataReference(projectId,
      MetadataReference.CreateFromFile(
          typeof(object).Assembly.Location))
    .AddMetadataReference(projectId,
      MetadataReference.CreateFromFile(
          typeof(Enumerable).Assembly.Location))
    .AddMetadataReference(projectId,
      MetadataReference.CreateFromFile(
          typeof(CSharpCompilation).Assembly.Location))
    .AddMetadataReference(projectId,
      MetadataReference.CreateFromFile(
          typeof(Compilation).Assembly.Location))
    .AddMetadataReference(projectId,
      MetadataReference.CreateFromFile(
          typeof(MustInvokeAttribute).Assembly.Location));

  var documentId = DocumentId.CreateNewId(projectId);
  solution = solution.AddDocument(documentId, "Test.cs",
    SourceText.From(code));

  return solution.GetProject(projectId).Documents.First();
}
```

We need to get a Document object, and the simplest way is to do that through an AdHocWorkspace (I'll discuss workspaces in Chapter 3). We add a project to the workspace's CurrentSolution with the appropriate metadata references. Then, we add a C# document to the project based on the given text, and return that document to the caller.

If we need to test for the existence of a diagnostic, Listing 2-11 shows what that looks like.

Listing 2-11. Testing for the presence of a diagnostic

```
[TestMethod]
[Case("Case3")]
public async Task Case3()
{
  await TestHelpers.RunAnalysisAsync<MustInvokeBaseMethodAnalyzer>(
    $@"Targets\{nameof(MustInvokeBaseMethodAnalyzerTests)}\Case3.cs",
    new[] { "MUST0001" }, diagnostics =>
    {
      Assert.AreEqual(1, diagnostics.Count(), nameof(Enumerable.Count));
      var diagnostic = diagnostics[0];
      var span = diagnostic.Location.SourceSpan;
      Assert.AreEqual(276, span.Start, nameof(span.Start));
      Assert.AreEqual(282, span.End, nameof(span.End));
    });
}
```

In this test method, we're testing the case in which an overriden method isn't invoking the base method like it should. Now we get a diagnostic coming back from the compilation, and we can test that we only get one diagnostic back with its location being the identifier of the method in the subclass. Because we have the code for the test in a C# file in the test project, we can easily use the Syntax Visualizer to find the Start and End values for the span of the diagnostic, as Figure 2-8 shows.

```
▷ OpenBraceToken [250..251]
▲ MethodDeclaration [255..313]
  ▷ PublicKeyword [255..261]
  ▷ OverrideKeyword [262..270]
  ▷ PredefinedType [271..275]
    IdentifierToken [276..282]
  ▷ ParameterList [282..284]
  ▷ Block [288..313]
```

```
0 references
public override void Method()
{
    base.Method();
}
```

Figure 2-8. *Using the Syntax Visualizer to get span values*

We also need tests for the code fix. Unlike the analyzer, we can assume that the code fix will only be invoked if there was an issue. However, we have a couple of cases to ensure we handle arguments and return values correctly. Again, the source code has all of the tests cases, but we'll just cover one here. Listing 2-12 has the test that covers if a base method invocation with no arguments and no return value was added correctly.

Listing 2-12. Verifying that a code fix works correctly

```
[TestMethod]
[Case("Case0")]
public async Task VerifyGetFixes()
{
  var code = File.ReadAllText(
```

```
  $@"Targets\{nameof(MustInvokeBaseMethodCallMethodCodeFixTests)}\Case0.cs");
var document = TestHelpers.Create(code);
var tree = await document.GetSyntaxTreeAsync();
var diagnostics = await TestHelpers.GetDiagnosticsAsync(
  code, new MustInvokeBaseMethodAnalyzer());
var sourceSpan = diagnostics[0].Location.SourceSpan;

var actions = new List<CodeAction>();
var codeActionRegistration =
  new Action<CodeAction, ImmutableArray<Diagnostic>>(
    (a, _) => { actions.Add(a); });

var fix = new MustInvokeBaseMethodCallMethodCodeFix();
var codeFixContext = new CodeFixContext(document, diagnostics[0],
  codeActionRegistration, new CancellationToken(false));
await fix.RegisterCodeFixesAsync(codeFixContext);

Assert.AreEqual(1, actions.Count, nameof(actions.Count));

await TestHelpers.VerifyActionAsync(actions,
  "Add base invocation", document,
  tree, new[]
    {
      "\r\n            {\r\n                base.Method();\r\n            }\r\n
    "});
}
```

As with the analyzer test, we create a diagnostic via GetDiagnosticsAsync(). This time, we use that diagnostic to create a CodeFixContext. This is passed into the code fix's RegisterCodeFixesAsync(). The Action<CodeAction, ImmutableArray<Diagnostic>> instance that we pass into the context is used to capture any registered actions with the code fix, which we can use to verify what we expect to happen in this test. The text that is passed into VerifyActionAsync() is the changed text that we expect to see in the new syntax tree. Here's what VerifyActionAsync() does.

```
internal static async Task VerifyActionAsync(List<CodeAction> actions,
  string title, Document document,
  SyntaxTree tree, string[] expectedNewTexts)
{
  var action = actions.Where(_ => _.Title == title).First();

  var operation = (await action.GetOperationsAsync(
    new CancellationToken(false))).ToArray()[0] as ApplyChangesOperation;
  var newDoc = operation.ChangedSolution.GetDocument(document.Id);
  var newTree = await newDoc.GetSyntaxTreeAsync();
  var changes = newTree.GetChanges(tree);
```

```
Assert.AreEqual(expectedNewTexts.Length, changes.Count,
  nameof(changes.Count));

foreach (var expectedNewText in expectedNewTexts)
{
  Assert.IsTrue(changes.Any(_ => _.NewText == expectedNewText),
    string.Join($"{Environment.NewLine}{Environment.NewLine}",
    changes.Select(_ => $"Change text: {_.NewText}")));
}
}
```

With these tests in place, we have a high level of confidence in our code and how it should behave. The next section discusses testing our diagnostic code within Visual Studio.

VSIX Installation

Unit tests are great, but you still need to run integration and end-to-end testing to make sure that the code works in the environment where it will really run. As you saw in the "Executing the Diagnostic and Code Fix" section, you can use the VSIX project to automatically install the analyzers and code fixes in a separate instance of Visual Studio. You can also run the code under the debugger so you can set breakpoints and see what your code is doing when Visual Studio invokes it.

Keep in mind that your code may stop at certain points if you use the CancellationToken to exit a method if cancellation was requested. Also, Visual Studio may end up calling your code multiple times from different threads, so the debugger may jump around a bit as you step through code. If you use the VSIX project for debugging, try to keep your sample code that you use for testing small, or comment out most of your sample code if you're narrowing your focus to one specific case. It'll make the debugging experience easier.

One other issue I've seen with the VSIX project is that, sometimes, your extension won't be updated, even if you update your code. There's no hard and fast rule as to when or why this happens, but if you notice that your analyzer or code fix code isn't firing when you thought it should, you may want to uninstall your extension. To do this, go to Tools ➤ Extensions and Updates. You should see a screen like the one in Figure 2-9.

Figure 2-9. *Finding your extension in Visual Studio*

Select your extension and click Uninstall. Close that instance of Visual Studio, and run your VSIX project again. That usually takes care of most update issues that I've seen when I use the extension.

Visual Studio Logging

Even with thorough testing, it's still possible that a developer can do something in their code that you didn't expect (for example, using a new feature in a new version of C#), and cause your code fix to crash because the expected syntax tree format is no longer valid. If it does, you'll get the "yellow bar of death" in Visual Studio that looks like what you see in Figure 2-10.

```
Class1.cs ⊨ ✕
ℹ 'ThrowsExceptionCodeFix' encountered an error and has been disabled.    [ Enable ]  [ Enable and ignore future errors ]
⊡ IntegrationTests                                                    ▾  ⁑⁎ IntegrationTests.Class1
      ⊟namespace IntegrationTests
      {
            0 references
      ⊟    public class Class1
            {
                  0 references
                  public void AMethod() { }

                  0 references
                  public int AnotherMethod() { return 44; }
      }                              ⊚ int Class1.AnotherMethod()
      }
                                     Returning ints is a really bad idea.
```

Figure 2-10. *Getting an error notification when a code fix fails*

The error that you see in Figure 2-10 was generated by a code fix in the ThrowsException sample code for this book. Its sole purpose is to report a diagnostic error whenever it runs into a method definition that returns an int:

```
[DiagnosticAnalyzer(LanguageNames.CSharp)]
public sealed class ThrowExceptionAnalyzer
  : DiagnosticAnalyzer
{
  private static DiagnosticDescriptor rule = new DiagnosticDescriptor(
    "THROW0001", "Returning Ints From Methods",
    "Returning ints is a really bad idea.",
    "Usage", DiagnosticSeverity.Error, true);

  public override ImmutableArray<DiagnosticDescriptor> SupportedDiagnostics
  {
    get
    {
      return ImmutableArray.Create(
        ThrowExceptionAnalyzer.rule);
    }
  }

  public override void Initialize(AnalysisContext context)
  {
    context.RegisterSyntaxNodeAction<SyntaxKind>(
      this.AnalyzeMethodDeclaration, SyntaxKind.MethodDeclaration);
  }

  private void AnalyzeMethodDeclaration(SyntaxNodeAnalysisContext context)
  {
    var method = context.Node as MethodDeclarationSyntax;
    var model = context.SemanticModel;
    var methodSymbol = model.GetDeclaredSymbol(method) as IMethodSymbol;
    var returnType = methodSymbol.ReturnType;
    var intType = typeof(int).GetTypeInfo();

    if (returnType.Name == intType.Name &&
      returnType.ContainingAssembly.Name == intType.Assembly.GetName().Name)
    {
      context.ReportDiagnostic(Diagnostic.Create(
        ThrowExceptionAnalyzer.rule,
        method.Identifier.GetLocation()));
    }
  }
}
```

The code fix, in turn, will immediately throw an exception:

```
[ExportCodeFixProvider(LanguageNames.CSharp)]
[Shared]
public sealed class ThrowsExceptionCodeFix
  : CodeFixProvider
{
  public override ImmutableArray<string> FixableDiagnosticIds
  {
    get
    {
      return ImmutableArray.Create("THROW0001");
    }
  }

  public override FixAllProvider GetFixAllProvider()
  {
    return WellKnownFixAllProviders.BatchFixer;
  }

  public override Task RegisterCodeFixesAsync(CodeFixContext context)
  {
    throw new NotSupportedException("I can't fix this!");
  }
}
```

As Figure 2-10 shows, Visual Studio immediately disables the analyzer—the developer has to choose to turn it back on via the Enable button. Note that Visual Studio does not exhibit the same behavior if a diagnostic throws an exception during its analysis—this only occurs for the code fix side of the equation.

This is nice in the sense that Visual Studio won't completely crash if a code fix keeps throwing exceptions due to bugs in the code base. However, the problem for the developer of the fix is, how do you get any diagnostic information about the exception? There's a command line switch that you can pass into Visual Studio when it launches called /log, which will write logging information to an XML file. Figure 2-11 shows what it looks like when you pass this switch into the command line.

Figure 2-11. *Launching Visual Studio with logging enabled*

■ **Note** For more information about using /log, see https://msdn.microsoft.com/en-us/library/ms241272.aspx.

Notice that if you use the Developer Command Prompt that's installed with Visual Studio 2015, you don't have to enter the path where Visual Studio's executable is located.

When you activate logging, the file is located at %APPDATA%\Microsoft\VisualStudio\Version\ActivityLog.xml. On my machine, I found it at C:\Users\jasonb\AppData\Roaming\Microsoft\VisualStudio\14.0. Here's a small sample of what you'll find in the file:

```xml
<?xml version="1.0" encoding="utf-16"?>
<?xml-stylesheet type="text/xsl" href="ActivityLog.xsl"?>
<activity>
  <entry>
    <record>1</record>
    <time>2016/01/17 15:39:29.523</time>
    <type>Information</type>
    <source>VisualStudio</source>
    <description>Microsoft Visual Studio 2015 version: 14.0.24720.0</description>
  </entry>
  <entry>
    <record>2</record>
    <time>2016/01/17 15:39:29.523</time>
    <type>Information</type>
    <source>VisualStudio</source>
    <description>Creating PkgDefCacheNonVolatile</description>
  </entry>
```

If a developer is experiencing problems with your code fix, they can invoke logging and hopefully obtain some exception information for you. Here's what I see when `ThrowsExceptionCodeFix` fails:

```xml
<entry>
  <record>544</record>
  <time>2016/01/17 15:45:09.078</time>
  <type>Error</type>
  <source>ThrowsExceptionCodeFix</source>
  <description>I can&apos;t fix this!&#x000D;&#x000A; at MustInvokeBaseMethod.
  Analyzers.ThrowsExceptionCodeFix.RegisterCodeFixesAsync(CodeFixContext
  context) in M:\JasonBock\Personal\Code Projects\CompilerAPIBook\
  Chapter 2\ThrowsException\ThrowsException\ThrowsExceptionCodeFix.
  cs:line 30&#x000D;&#x000A; at Microsoft.CodeAnalysis.CodeFixes.
  CodeFixService.&lt;&gt;c__DisplayClass19_1.&lt;ContainsAnyFix&gt;b__1()&#x000D;
  &#x000A; at Microsoft.CodeAnalysis.Extensions.IExtensionManagerExtensions.&lt;
  PerformActionAsync&gt;d__2.MoveNext()</description>
</entry>
```

You can see in the call stack that the exception is at line 30 of the ThrowsExceptionCodeFix.cs file. It would be helpful if Visual Studio also logged the file and location in the developer's code where the code fix was executed as that would help figure out why the code fix is failing. But at least this location gives you a starting point to track down the problem.

One last point about debugging. If you want to run Visual Studio with logging enabled while you're debugging your code fix, you need to change one property of the VSIX project. Go to the project's properties, then go to the Debug tab. In the Start Options section, change the Command Line Arguments to what you see in Figure 2-12.

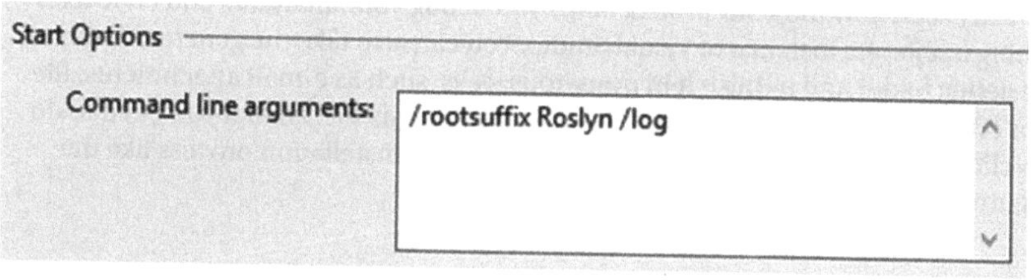

Start Options

Command line arguments: /rootsuffix Roslyn /log

Figure 2-12. Changing VSIX command line options to enable debugging

By the way, the /rootsuffix option launches Visual Studio in an "experimental" mode. That means that your VSIX isn't installed into your normal space. You can verify this by looking at installed extensions in Visual Studio when you launch it normally in Windows—you won't see the VSIX package in that list. But as you saw in Figure 2-9, you will see it in the experimental instance. This is beneficial because it keeps potentially buggy code isolated from other Visual Studio modes. However, it does change where the log file is stored. In my case, it looks like this: C:\Users\jasonb\AppData\Roaming\Microsoft\VisualStudio\14.0Roslyn. Note the change in the version part of the path. It includes "Roslyn" in the path because that name was included in the command line argument for /rootsuffix. You can choose to make your own experimental modes if you'd like, just make sure you keep track of what got installed in it.

■ **Note** For more information about launching Visual Studio in an "experimental" mode, see https://msdn.microsoft.com/en-us/library/bb166560.aspx.

The last part of the diagnostic puzzle is deployment and installation, so you know how developers can use your diagnostics and code fixes. That's what we'll explore in the final section of this chapter.

Deploying and Installing Diagnostics

So far, all of the code I've shown in this chapter has run on one machine. We want other developers to use the code we've written without a lot of work. For deployment and installation there are two options available: VSIX and NuGet packages. Let's start with extensions.

VSIX Packaging

You've already seen how the VSIX project helps you debug your analyzers and code fixes by launching a separate instance of Visual Studio. You can also take the generated .vsix file in the debug folder and publish it in numerous ways, such as e-mail attachments, file servers, or even the Visual Studio Gallery. If you have the .vsix file, all that you need to do is double-click on the file, and it'll automatically kick in an installation process like the one in Figure 2-13.

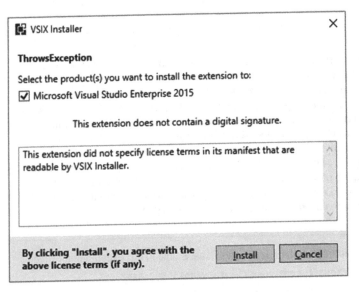

Figure 2-13. Installing an extension from the file

Note For more details about publishing a Visual Studio extension, see `https://msdn.microsoft.com/en-us/library/ff728613.aspx`.

Keep in mind when you're using a diagnostic that's installed with a VSIX that any errors reported by a diagnostic will not be included in the build such that the build fails. Figure 2-14 shows you the Error window when the `MustInvokeBaseMethodAnalzyer` reports an issue.

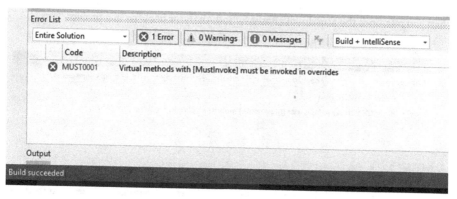

Figure 2-14. Successful build even with diagnostic errors

Even though there's an error in the list, the build says it's successful. Personally, I don't like this behavior. If a diagnostic is reporting a problem, but the build is successful, I probably won't check the Error list.

Also, when you install a diagnostic via a VSIX, that diagnostic will run for every project that you load in Visual Studio. For some diagnostics, this may be too coarse-grained, especially if it's tied to a specific framework that you only use in specific projects. However, if the diagnostic is one that enforces an idiom with the .NET Framework that you want all developers on your team to adhere to, this may be the right approach.

The other installation option is a NuGet package.

NuGet Packaging

NuGet has become the standard way of sharing and installing assemblies in .NET. You can find a myriad of packages that cover all sorts of aspects in software development: logging, business rules, dependency injection containers, and so on. With diagnostics, you can also publish your analyzers as a NuGet package. The analyzer project template will create the necessary PowerShell scripts and the .nuspec file to create the package when you build the project. You'll find a .nupkg file in the appropriate subfolder of the \bin folder. Publish that file to either Nuget.org or a local NuGet repository, and you're done.

■ **Note**   If you change the name of the .nuspec file, you'll have to manually change a postbuild step in the project file. Open the project file in a text editor (or unload it in Visual Studio and edit it there), and look in the `Target` element with the `Name` attribute set to `AfterBuild`. You'll see the .nuspec file being passed into an invocation of NuGet.exe. Change the name and then you won't get any postbuild errors.

To contrast this NuGet package installation option with the VSIX approach, errors reported from a diagnostic will cause a build to fail. Figure 2-15 shows how this works when you reference the MustInvokeBaseMethod.Analyzer package in a project.

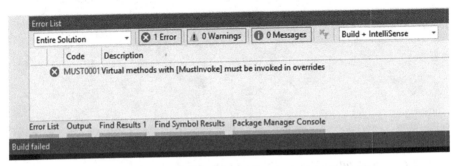

Figure 2-15. *Analyzers failing from a NuGet installation will fail the build*

With a NuGet installation, however, remember that it's per-project. You can install a NuGet package across an entire solution, but if you add projects to the solution after that, you'll still need to remember to install the NuGet package into these new projects.

Conclusion

This chapter covered how diagnostics work in the Compiler API and the importance of designing the analyzers and code fixes. I also discussed how they're all implemented, tested, debugged, and published. In the next chapter, we'll move on to refactorings and workspaces.

CHAPTER 3

Creating Refactorings and Handling Workspaces

In this chapter, we'll spend time investigating refactorings in the Compiler API. You'll learn how they work and what you need to do to implement one. Because refactorings tend to use a fair amount of members in the Workspaces API, we'll examine that as well.

Consistency in Structure

If there's one term that is the most misused term in software development, it's arguably "refactoring." Most of the time when a developer talks about "refactoring code," they're making a number of changes to the code that break existing functionality. While that may be something that must be done to streamline the code base or make performance better, that's really not what refactoring is. Here's what I consider to be the official definition of refactoring:

> *Refactoring is the process of changing a software system in such a way that it does not alter the external behavior of the code yet improves its internal structure.*

> —Martin Fowler, "Refactoring," 1999, pg, xvi

For example, consider the code in Listing 3-1.

Listing 3-1. Performing a simple arithmetic calculation

```
using System;
using System.Collections.Generic;
using System.Linq;
using System.Text;
using System.Threading.Tasks;
```

```
namespace SimpleExamples
{
  class Program
  {
    static void Main(string[] args)
    {
      decimal value = 0;

      if(args.Length > 0 && decimal.TryParse(args[0], out value))
      {
        var initialValue = value * 2;
        var nextValue = initialValue + 3;
        var finalValue = (value * 3) - (nextValue / 2) + 2;
        Console.Out.WriteLine("Final value: ");
        Console.Out.WriteLine(finalValue.ToString());
      }
    }
  }
}
```

It's a small piece of code that does a simple calculation: 3*x - (2*x + 3) / 2 + 2. The code is based on what Visual Studio generates when you add a new class to a project. If I pass in 3 to the console app, it'll print out 7 as the answer. Is there any way we can refactor the code so it's a little cleaner?

Visual Studio has some built-in refactorings that we can use in this code. If we highlight the first three lines in the if statement, we can press Ctrl + . (period), and access the "Extract Method" refactoring, as shown in Figure 3-1.

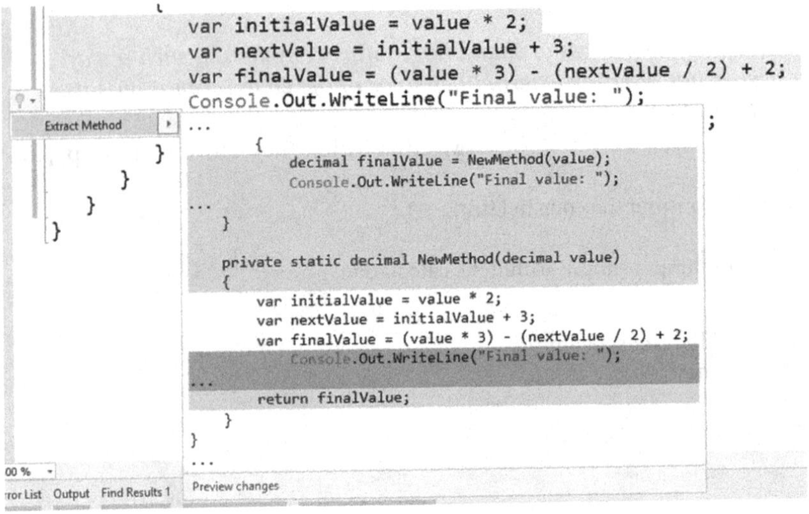

Figure 3-1. *Using the Extract Method refactoring*

If I accept this refactoring, the code change is made. Visual Studio then puts me into the Rename refactoring to give me the opportunity to change the default name of the generated method, "NewMethod". This is the same mode you would get if you pressed F2 on a code member. The Rename refactor is shown in Figure 3-2.

```
if(args.Length > 0 && decimal.TryParse(args[0], out value))
{
    decimal finalValue = NewMethod(value);
    Console.Out.WriteLine("Final value: ");
    Console.Out.WriteLine(finalValue.ToString());
}
}
```

Rename: NewMethod ✕
Modify any highlighted location to begin renaming.
☐ Include comments
☐ Include strings
☐ Preview changes
Rename will update 2 references in 1 file.
[Apply]

```
1 reference
private static decimal NewMethod(decimal value)
{
    var initialValue = value * 2;
    var nextValue = initialValue + 3;
    var finalValue = (value * 3) - (nextValue / 2) + 2;
    return finalValue;
}
```

Figure 3-2. *Using the Rename refactoring*

Then I rename the method to Calculate(). Now this calculation is isolated into its own method, so any updates can be made here rather than in the console's Main() method. In fact, this calculation can be refactored to 2 * value + 0.5, so if I update the implementation of the method, any callers of Calculate() will automatically get that change.

We can also pull out the string "Final Value: ", which is passed into WriteLine(), and put it into a constant, as shown in Figure 3-3.

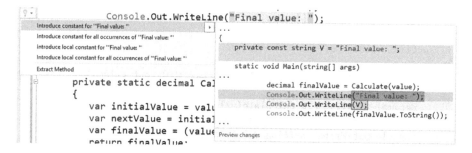

Figure 3-3. *Creating a constant value via a refactoring*

Finally, as Figure 3-4 shows, we can remove a bunch of using statements that have no value.

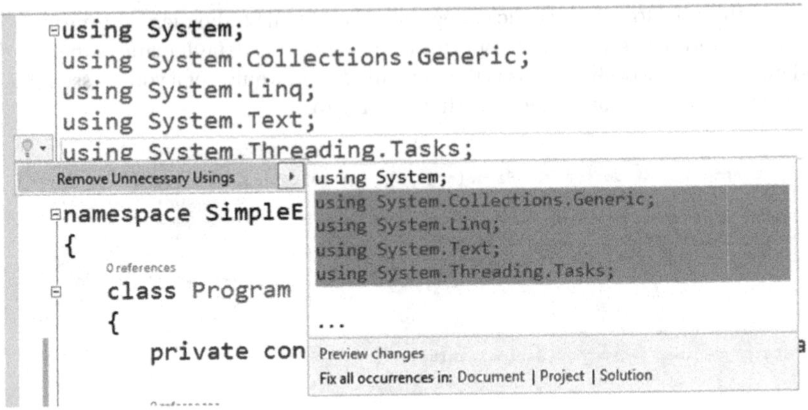

Figure 3-4. Removing unnecessary using statements

With all these updates in place, Listing 3-2 shows what the code looks like now.

Listing 3-2. Refactoring the simple arithmetic calculation

```
using System;

namespace SimpleExamples
{
  class Program
  {
    private const string FinalValueMessage = "Final value: ";

    static void Main(string[] args)
    {
      decimal value = 0;

      if(args.Length > 0 && decimal.TryParse(args[0], out value))
      {
        decimal finalValue = Calculate(value);
        Console.Out.WriteLine(FinalValueMessage);
        Console.Out.WriteLine(finalValue.ToString());
      }
    }

    private static decimal Calculate(decimal value)
    {
      return 2 * value + 0.5M;
    }
  }
}
```

Compare the original implementation in Listing 3-1 with the modifications in Listing 3-2. We have nearly the same number of lines of code, but we have better organization and structure to the code, with less noise to boot. This is exactly what refactoring is, and having tools built into to a developer's IDE makes running refactorings painless.

But a tool vendor can't provide all the refactoring that the majority of developers would like to use. Although Visual Studio, as you just saw, has some refactorings in place, there may other refactorings that you'd love to introduce into its system without having to wait for Microsoft to create it or for third-party tool vendors to add more to their product, if they ever will. However, with the Compiler API and its integration into Visual Studio, you can define your own refactorings whenever you want. As you saw in Chapter 2, it's fairly straightfoward to create an analyzer and code fix; the same is true of a refactoring. Let's walk through creating a custom refactoring in Visual Studio that moves all the types from a file into their own files.

Developing a Refactoring

In this section, we'll explore how a refactoring is made. We'll examine its design first, and then go through the steps needed to implement the refactoring.

Understanding the Problem

The refactoring we're going to make in this chapter is centered on the idea that every class should have its own file, that is, if I have code like this in a .cs file:

```
public class One { /* ... */ }
public class Two { /* ... */ }
public class Three { /* ... */ }
```

What I'd like to have is three separate files called One.cs, Two.cs, and Three.cs. If these classes had any nested classes, they'd just come along for the ride.

But consider this code scenario:

```
public class One { /* ... */ }
public class Two { /* ... */ }

namespace SubNamespace
{
  public class Three { /* ... */ }
}
```

What I'd do in this case is have a subfolder called SubNamespace and put Three.cs in that folder. In other words, if the following code structure exists, the resulting folder structure should look like Figure 3-5:

```
namespace Company.Product.Core
{
    public class One { /* ... */ }
    public class Two { /* ... */ }

    namespace SubNamespace
    {
        public class Three { /* ... */ }
    }
}
```

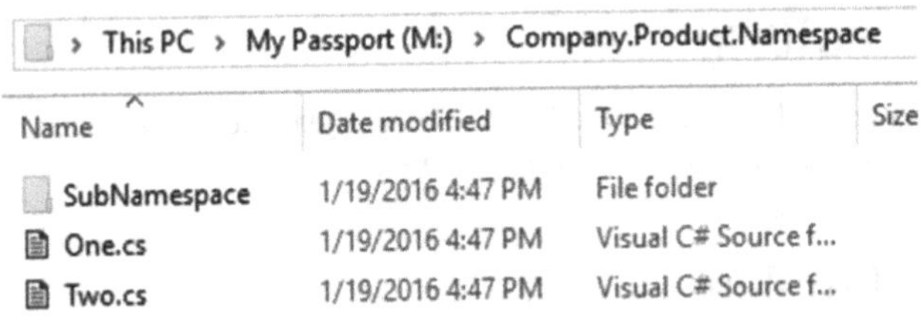

Name	Date modified	Type	Size
SubNamespace	1/19/2016 4:47 PM	File folder	
One.cs	1/19/2016 4:47 PM	Visual C# Source f...	
Two.cs	1/19/2016 4:47 PM	Visual C# Source f...	

This PC > My Passport (M:) > Company.Product.Namespace

Figure 3-5. *Folder structure for code files (assume that Three.cs exists in the SubNamespace folder)*

Of course, the original file would be deleted unless it was already named One.cs or Two.cs. We'd have to be careful to only clean up the original file if it was no longer needed. But what about using directives? What if there were 5 using directives at the top, but only 3 were needed for the code in One.cs, 2 were needed for Two.cs, and all 5 were needed for Three.cs? What about developers who don't follow this namespace to folder mapping convention for file storage? Perhaps our refactoring should provide an option to just create the new files in the current directory and let developers move them around wherever they want to after that. Also, what if the filenames Two.cs and Three.cs already exist? We don't want to overwrite what's currently there.

With this scenario in mind, let's create a refactoring that will provide two options to the user if there are more than 1 top-level classes in that file. One option is to create files with the folder convention shown in Figure 3-5. The other option is to simply create the files in the same directory as the current file. In both cases, we need to be careful not to create name collisions with new files and we'll only include the necessary using statements in the new files. In the next section, we'll set up all of the Visual Studio projects needed to create this refactoring.

Creating a Refactoring Solution

In the "Using the Template" section in Chapter 2, we used a template to create the analyzer projects. There's a similar template for refactorings, as shown in Figure 3-6.

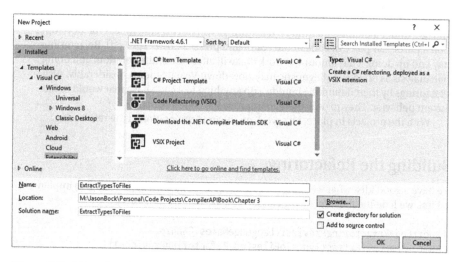

Figure 3-6. *Using the refactoring project template*

When you click OK, you'll get the solution layout shown in Figure 3-7.

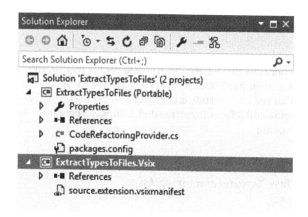

Figure 3-7. *Refactoring projects that are generated by the template*

As with the analyzer template, a somewhat silly example is generated that offers a refactoring for any class to reverse its name. For example, a class named "Customer" would be changed to "remotsuC" if this refactoring was used. But, as with the generated analyzer example, it's worth perusing the code to get familiar with its setup and check

out some of the methods you might want to use in the refactorings that you create (like
Renamer.RenameSymbolAsync(), which does a symbol rename for you across a solution).
Also, note that there is no test project made with the template. We'll fix that problem in
the "Unit Testing" section later in this chapter.

Note that I keep using the phrase "offer a refactoring." Unlike an analyzer, which
will immediately show a visual indicator in Visual Studio if an issue is present (e.g., a red
squiggle under a method identifier), refactorings will not execute unless the developer
is on a particular piece of code in the editor and presses Ctrl + . (period). Refactorings
may end up doing a fair amount of work that will affect the entire solution, and doing
that analysis as often as a diagnostic may slow down Visual Studio considerably. Also,
refactorings by their defintion shouldn't do anything to a code base that would break
current behavior. They're only there to improve the code's structure.

With the projects in place, let's work on the implementation of the refactoring.

Building the Refactoring

We have a good idea what we want to do with our refactoring. Now we need to implement
it. First, we'll define the refactoring class:

```
[ExportCodeRefactoringProvider(LanguageNames.CSharp,
  Name = nameof(ExtractTypesToFilesCodeRefactoringProvider))]
[Shared]
internal class ExtractTypesToFilesCodeRefactoringProvider
  : CodeRefactoringProvider
{
  public sealed override async Task ComputeRefactoringsAsync(
    CodeRefactoringContext context)
  {
    /* ... */
```

Similar to analyzers, we adorn our class that inherits from CodeRefactoringProvider
with a couple of attributes so environments like Visual Studio can identify them and use
them correctly. The only member that you can override is ComputeRefactoringsAsync(),
which is where you'll use the context to add refactorings if needed. Listing 3-3 contains
the overridden method's implementation.

Listing 3-3. Implementing ComputeRefactoringsAsync() in a refactoring class

```
public sealed override async Task ComputeRefactoringsAsync(
  CodeRefactoringContext context)
{
  var document = context.Document;
  var documentFileNameWithoutExtension =
    Path.GetFileNameWithoutExtension(document.FilePath);
```

```
var root = await document.GetSyntaxRootAsync(context.CancellationToken)
  .ConfigureAwait(false);
var model = await document.GetSemanticModelAsync(
  context.CancellationToken)
  .ConfigureAwait(false);

var typesToRemove = root.GetTypesToRemove(
  model, documentFileNameWithoutExtension);

if(typesToRemove.Length > 1)
{
  context.RegisterRefactoring(CodeAction.Create(
    "Move types to files in folders",
    async token => await CreateFiles(
      document, root, model, typesToRemove,
      _ => _.Replace(".", "\\"), token)));
  context.RegisterRefactoring(CodeAction.Create(
    "Move types to files in current folder",
    async token => await CreateFiles(
      document, root, model, typesToRemove,
      _ => string.Empty, token)));
  }
}
```

We'll check the root node from the given Document object and see how many top level types exist in the document. That's what's done in GetTypesToRemove(), which is implemented in Listing 3-4.

Listing 3-4. Calculating the types to remove from the file

```
internal static ImmutableArray<TypeToRemove> GetTypesToRemove(
  this SyntaxNode @this, SemanticModel model,
  string documentFileNameWithoutExtension)
{
  var typesToRemove = new List<TypeToRemove>();
  TypeDeclarationSyntax typeToPreserve = null;

  var typeNodes = @this.DescendantNodes(_ => true)
    .OfType<TypeDeclarationSyntax>();

  foreach(var typeNode in typeNodes)
  {
    var type = model.GetDeclaredSymbol(typeNode) as ITypeSymbol;

    if(type.ContainingType == null)
    {
      if(type.Name != documentFileNameWithoutExtension)
      {
```

```
      typesToRemove.Add(new TypeToRemove(
        typeNode, type));
    }
    else
    {
      typeToPreserve = typeNode;
    }
  }
}

return typesToRemove.ToImmutableArray();
}
```

We only want to move types to other files if they're not nested types and they don't have the same name as the current document's file name. The TypeToRemove class is a simple, immutable object that contains the TypeDeclarationSyntax and ITypeSymbol objects for a given type declaration:

```
internal sealed class TypeToRemove
{
  public TypeToRemove(TypeDeclarationSyntax declaration,
    ITypeSymbol symbol)
  {
    this.Declaration = declaration;
    this.Symbol = symbol;
  }

  public TypeDeclarationSyntax Declaration { get; }
  public ITypeSymbol Symbol { get; }
}
```

If there's more than one type, we provide two refactorings: one that puts files into separate folders if necessary, the other puts the files into the current directory. CreateFiles() is where we create new files and update the current one so it doesn't contained the moved types. Listing 3-5 shows how it works.

Listing 3-5. Creating new files for types

```
private static async Task<Solution> CreateFiles(Document document,
  SyntaxNode root, SemanticModel model,
  ImmutableArray<TypeToRemove> typesToRemove,
  Func<string, string> typeFolderGenerator, CancellationToken token)
{
  var project = document.Project;
  var workspace = project.Solution.Workspace;
```

```
project = MoveTypeNodes(
  model, typesToRemove, typeFolderGenerator, project, token);

var newRoot = root.RemoveNodes(
  typesToRemove.Select(_ => _.Declaration),
  SyntaxRemoveOptions.AddElasticMarker);

var newSolution = project.Solution;
var projectId = project.Id;
newSolution = newSolution.WithDocumentSyntaxRoot(document.Id, newRoot);

var newDocument = newSolution.GetProject(
  project.Id).GetDocument(document.Id);
newRoot = await newDocument.GetSyntaxRootAsync(token);
var newModel = await newDocument.GetSemanticModelAsync(token);
var newUsings = newRoot.GenerateUsingDirectives(newModel);

newRoot = newRoot.RemoveNodes(
  newRoot.DescendantNodes(_ => true).OfType<UsingDirectiveSyntax>(),
  SyntaxRemoveOptions.AddElasticMarker);

newRoot = (newRoot as CompilationUnitSyntax)?.WithUsings(newUsings);
  return newSolution.WithDocumentSyntaxRoot(document.Id, newRoot);
}
```

Most of the implementation lies within MoveTypeNodes()—we'll get back to that one in a moment. After we move the types to different files, we then remove all of the type declarations with RemoveNodes(). Then, we update the current document with our new SyntaxNode and subsequently the current Solution. Remember, whenever you think you're changing an object within the Compiler API it usually doesn't change that specific object reference because it's probably immutable. The last thing we do is remove all of the existing using statements and add only the ones we need. This list is generated with GenerateUsingDirectives(), as shown in Listing 3-6.

Listing 3-6. Creating all the necessary using statements for a type

```
internal static SyntaxList<UsingDirectiveSyntax> GenerateUsingDirectives(
  this SyntaxNode @this, SemanticModel model)
{
  var namespacesForType = new SortedSet<string>();

  foreach (var childNode in @this.DescendantNodes(_ => true))
  {
    var symbol = model.GetSymbolInfo(childNode).Symbol;
```

```
    if (symbol != null && symbol.Kind != SymbolKind.Namespace &&
      symbol.ContainingNamespace != null)
    {
      if ((symbol as ITypeSymbol)?.SpecialType ==
        SpecialType.System_Void)
      {
        continue;
      }

      var containingNamespace = symbol.GetContainingNamespace();

      if (!string.IsNullOrWhiteSpace(containingNamespace))
      {
        namespacesForType.Add(containingNamespace);
      }
    }
  }
}

  return SyntaxFactory.List(
    namespacesForType.Select(_ => SyntaxFactory.UsingDirective(
      SyntaxFactory.IdentifierName(_))));
}
```

We go through all of the descendant nodes in the given node, and if the given node has a symbol that isn't void and has a containing namespace that doesn't end up being an empty string (i.e., the global namespace), we add it to our list. This list is used to generate UsingDirectiveSyntax objects. By the way, most .NET developers don't use or think about the global namespace. There's always a "global" namespace: type "global" in Visual Studio and you'll see all the top-level namespaces within it, as Figure 3-8 shows.

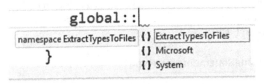

Figure 3-8. *Using the global namespace in C#*

In the Compiler API, that global namespace will have an empty string for its Name, so we have to ignore that one.

Let's go back to MoveTypeNodes(), as this is really where the essence of the refactoring exists. This method's implementation is shown in Listing 3-7.

Listing 3-7. Moving types into specific files

```
private static Project MoveTypeNodes(SemanticModel model,
  ImmutableArray<TypeToRemove> typesToRemove,
  Func<string, string> typeFolderGenerator, Project project,
  CancellationToken token)
{
  var projectDirectory = Path.GetDirectoryName(project.FilePath);
  var projectName = project.Name;

  foreach (var typeToRemove in typesToRemove)
  {
    token.ThrowIfCancellationRequested();
    var fileName = $"{typeToRemove.Symbol.Name}.cs";

    var containingNamespace = typeToRemove.Symbol.GetContainingNamespace();
    var typeFolder = typeFolderGenerator(containingNamespace).Replace(
      projectName, string.Empty);

    if (typeFolder.StartsWith("\\"))
    {
      typeFolder = typeFolder.Remove(0, 1);
    }

    var fileLocation = Path.Combine(projectDirectory, typeFolder);

    project = project.AddDocument(fileName,
      typeToRemove.Declaration.GetCompilationUnitForType(
          model, containingNamespace),
      folders: !string.IsNullOrWhiteSpace(typeFolder) ?
        new[] { typeFolder } : null).Project;
  }
  return project;
}
```

We create a new file for the project with the Project's AddDocument() method. A new CompilationUnitSyntax object is created for that document, which will contain just that type and relevant using statements. The typeFolder variable is used to put the document into a subfolder depending on what the typeFolderGenerator Func returns.

■ **Note** You shouldn't pass in a blank value into the folders argument; you'll get a COMException if you do. At least, this is the behavior that I saw. There's no explicit documentation I found on what would happen if I did that; I found out by accident. The Compiler API doesn't have a large volume of documentation on it unless you're willing to spelunk through its code base, and that's not always a trivial endeavor. That's why unit and integration testing is essential to creating stable analyzers and diagnostics.

Here's how the new `CompilationUnitSyntax` is created:

```
internal static CompilationUnitSyntax GetCompilationUnitForType(
  this MemberDeclarationSyntax @this,
  SemanticModel model, string containingNamespace)
{
  var usingsForType = @this.GenerateUsingDirectives(model);

  return SyntaxFactory.CompilationUnit()
    .WithUsings(usingsForType)
    .WithMembers(
      SyntaxFactory.SingletonList<MemberDeclarationSyntax>(
        SyntaxFactory.NamespaceDeclaration(
          SyntaxFactory.IdentifierName(containingNamespace))
        .WithMembers(
          SyntaxFactory.List<MemberDeclarationSyntax>(
                      new[] { @this }))))
    .WithAdditionalAnnotations(Formatter.Annotation);
}
```

We use `GenerateUsingDirectives()` to only get the using directives for this declaration. Then we create a `CompilationUnitSyntax` with those new using directives, a `NamespaceDeclarationSyntax` for the type, and the type itself.

Now that we have the code in place, let's run it in Visual Studio and see what it does.

Executing the Refactoring

With the refactoring class finished, it's time to see what it will do in Visual Studio. Just like the analzyer template you saw in the "Using the Template" section in Chapter 2, a VSIX project is created that will install your refactoring into a separate hive of Visual Studio. Make that VSIX project the startup project, run it, and create a new class library project in the new Visual Studio instance. Add this code to the Class1.cs file:

```
using System;
using System.Collections.Generic;
using System.IO;
using System.Linq;
using System.Text;
using System.Threading.Tasks;

namespace IntegrationTests
{
  public class Class1
  {
    public void DoIt(Stream stream) { }
    public class Class4 { }
  }
```

```
public class Class2
{
  public Guid ProduceThis(Stream stream)
  {
    return Guid.NewGuid();
  }
}

namespace SubNamespace
{
  public class Class3
  {
  }
}
}
```

What the code does isn't really important. We're more interested in how our refactoring will move the type defintions around. This code allows us to test our refactoring scenarios.

To invoke the refactoring, place the cursor anywhere in the code file. Press Ctrl + . (period), and you should see options like those in Figure 3-9.

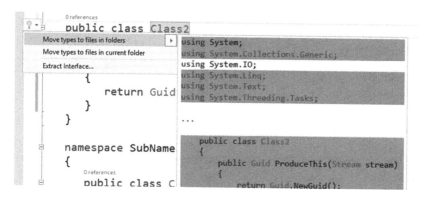

Figure 3-9. Getting the refactorings to show up in Visual Studio

You might see more options based on what member the cursor is on from other refactorings setup in Visual Studio, but the two refactoring options we create ("Move types to files in folders" and "Move types to files in current folder") should be in the list.

The diff window now shows that we'll be deleting a lot of code, but it doesn't show where that code will go. That's one minor disadvantage with what our refactorings do in that you don't see a difference between the project and solution, and there will be! Figure 3-10 shows what the current folder structure looks like before we apply any refactorings.

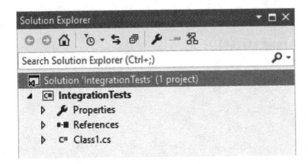

Figure 3-10. *The project before the refactoring*

After we accept the changes, Figure 3-11 shows what happens to the project.

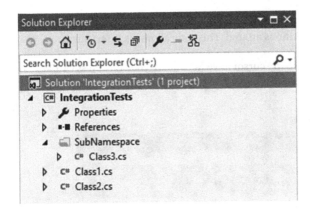

Figure 3-11. *The project after the refactoring*

Notice that the definition of Class1 stays in Class1.cs. Here's what the contents of that file is now:

```
using System.IO;

namespace IntegrationTests
{
  public class Class1
  {
    public void DoIt(Stream stream) { }
    public class Class4 { }
  }
```

```
namespace SubNamespace
    {
    }
}
```

Irrelevant using directives are gone; only Class1 remains.

Visual Studio also uses the convention of adding a numeric value after a file name if you try to add a file with a name that already exists. For example, if a file called Class2.cs was in the root directory, Figure 3-12 shows what Visual Studio does with the file collision.

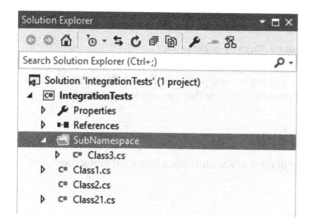

Figure 3-12. *Visual Studio handles file name collisions for you*

Because refactorings are in a PCL, there's no "File.Exists()" call you can use to determine if you'd make a duplicate file. Fortunately, Visual Studio handles duplicates for you.

The other refactoring, "Move types to files in current folder", doesn't make any subdirectories. Figure 3-13 shows what happens when that option is selected.

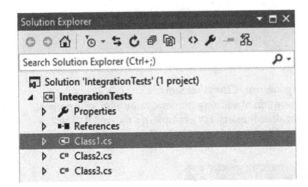

Figure 3-13. *Files are made in the same directory as the project*

We now have a refactoring that will move our types into different files for us. The next section explains how to test the refactoring to ensure that they work as expected.

Debugging Refactorings

In this section, you'll use two different ways to test and debug your refactoring code: unit testing and VSIX projects.

Unit Testing

As discussed in Chapter 2, unit testing is important to ensure your code works as expected. Surprisingly, the refactoring template doesn't create a unit test project for you, but it's easy to add one to the solution. We'll stick with an MSTest-based project to stay consistent with the analyzer examples, but NUnit or xUnit would work just fine. Right-click on the solution in the Solution Explorer, and select Add ➤ New Project. Select the Test node in the tree view on the left, and you should see a Unit Test Project option as shown in Figure 3-14.

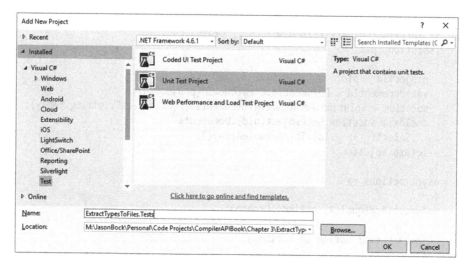

Figure 3-14. *Adding a testing project for the refactoring*

Once the project is made, add a reference to the refactoring project so you can test your code.

■ **Note**   You'll also need to add the right Compiler API packages. One way to make this slightly easier is to take the packages.config file from a test project created for a diagnostics project and put it into this test project. Also, you'll need to update the assembly references so the test project is referencing the Compiler API assemblies. Again, a manual but reliable way to do this is to copy the appropriate <Reference> elements from the diagnostic test project into the test project for the refactorings.

There's a lot of test cases to cover, and they're all in the sample code, but we'll just cover a couple in the book. One is when a document has classes to move that would cause a conflict; another is when there is only one class in the target document. Listing 3-8 has the test for the first scenario.

Listing 3-8. Testing for file collisions

```
[TestMethod]
public async Task RefactorWhenFileCollisionOccurs()
{
  ProjectId projectId = null;
  ImmutableArray<DocumentId> docIds;
  var folder = nameof(ExtractTypesToFilesCodeRefactoringProviderTests);
  var fileName = nameof(RefactorWhenFileCollisionOccurs);
```

```csharp
await TestHelpers.TestProvider(
  $@"Targets\{folder}\{fileName}.cs", "Class1.cs",
  (solution, pid) =>
  {
    projectId = pid;
    var documentId = DocumentId.CreateNewId(projectId);
    solution = solution.AddDocument(documentId, "Class2.cs", string.Empty);
    docIds = solution.GetProject(pid).Documents
      .Select(_ => _.Id).ToImmutableArray();
    return solution;
  },
  async actions =>
  {
    Assert.AreEqual(2, actions.Length);

    foreach (var action in actions)
    {
      var operations = await action.GetOperationsAsync(
        default(CancellationToken));
      Assert.AreEqual(1, operations.Length);

      var appliedOperation = (operations[0] as ApplyChangesOperation);
      var changedSolution = appliedOperation.ChangedSolution;
      var changedProject = changedSolution.GetProject(projectId);
      var changedDocuments = changedProject.Documents.Where(
        _ => !docIds.Any(id => id == _.Id)).ToImmutableArray();

      Assert.AreEqual(2, changedDocuments.Length);

      foreach (var document in changedDocuments)
      {
        var text = await document.GetTextAsync();
        var textValue = new StringBuilder();

        using (var writer = new StringWriter(textValue))
        {
          text.Write(writer);
        }

        var resultFile = $@"Targets\{folder}\{fileName}{document.Name}";
        Assert.AreEqual(File.ReadAllText(resultFile), textValue.ToString());
      }
    }
  });
}
```

There's a lot of code in the test from Listing 3-8, so let's start with the TestProvider():

```
internal static async Task TestProvider(string file, string fileName,
    Func<Solution, ProjectId, Solution> modifySolution,
    Func<ImmutableArray<CodeAction>, Task> handleActions)
{
    var code = File.ReadAllText(file);
    var document = TestHelpers.CreateDocument(code, fileName, modifySolution);
    var actions = new List<CodeAction>();
    var actionRegistration = new Action<CodeAction>(
        action => actions.Add(action));
    var context = new CodeRefactoringContext(document, new TextSpan(0, 1),
        actionRegistration, new CancellationToken(false));

    var provider = new ExtractTypesToFilesCodeRefactoringProvider();
    await provider.ComputeRefactoringsAsync(context);
    await handleActions(actions.ToImmutableArray());
}
```

TestProvider() is very similar to the helper method that we made for the diagnostic test. It loads code from a file that is passed into an instance of our refactoring, capturing any actions that the refactoring reports in ComputeRefactoringsAsync() via the actionRegistration Action. A modifySolution Func is also passed in to modify the generated solution from CreateDocument(). CreateDocument() is similar to the Create() method shown in the "Unit Testing" section in Chapter 2, so I won't cover that again. Just remember that it allows the tester to modify the solution if needed, and that's exactly what we need to do in our first test.

In the first lambda passed into TestProvider(), we add a second empty Document called Class2.cs. We also capture the project's identifier and a list of all document identifiers in the project. We use those in the second lambda, where we assert what the refactorings did. First, we check that we got two CodeAction values back. Then we check the operations associated with each CodeAction. We have to cast the operation to an ApplyChangesOperation. The base type, CodeActionOperation, doesn't provide as much information as ApplyChangesOperation, and we need that so we can look at the documents that changed. To get those documents, we have to remove the documents that were there before the refactoring made changes, which is what Where() is doing. We then compare the contents of these new documents with expected values that are stored in files within the Targets directory.

■ **Note**   It took some time to figure out how to set up the test code so I could verify behaviors. For example, casting to ApplyChangesOperation wasn't obvious at first. I had to debugging the test to see what the return value was providing, because if CodeActionOperation was all that was available, we wouldn't be able to meaningfully assert anything in our tests.

Now, you may be wondering why there wasn't a file named "Class21.cs" that was generated as we saw when we ran this code in Visual Studio. In "Interacting with a Workspace" I'll clarify that in more detail. For now, remember that we're using an AdHocWorksapce to generate our solution, project and documents; this is different than the one you use in Visual Studio. Therefore, behaviors can be different as our test shows: AdHocWorkspace doesn't generate a new file with a different name. It just overwrites the file that exists. However, at least we can check that our refactoring moves code around as expected.

The second test—having only one class in the target document—is much smaller:

```
[TestMethod]
public async Task RefactorWhenOnlyOneTypeIsDefined()
{
  var folder = nameof(ExtractTypesToFilesCodeRefactoringProviderTests);
  var fileName = nameof(RefactorWhenOnlyOneTypeIsDefined);

  await TestHelpers.TestProvider(
    $@"Targets\{folder}\{fileName}.cs", "Class1.cs",
    null,
    actions =>
    {
      Assert.AreEqual(0, actions.Length);
      return Task.CompletedTask;
    });
}
```

In this test, we only have one type definition in the source file, so we don't expect to get any CodeAction values generated from the refactoring.

We can also test our extension methods using the helper methods in TestHelpers. For example, here's the test for GenerateUsingExtensions():

```
[TestMethod]
public async Task GenerateUsingDirectives()
{
  var folder = nameof(SyntaxNodeExtensionsTests);
  var fileName = nameof(GenerateUsingDirectives);

  var document = TestHelpers.CreateDocument(
    File.ReadAllText($@"Targets\Extensions\{folder}\{fileName}.cs"),
    "Class1.cs", null);

  var root = await document.GetSyntaxRootAsync();
  var model = await document.GetSemanticModelAsync();

  var directives = root.GenerateUsingDirectives(model);
  Assert.AreEqual(3, directives.Count);
```

```
  directives.Single(_ => _.Name.ToString() == "System");
  directives.Single(_ => _.Name.ToString() == "System.IO");
  directives.Single(_ => _.Name.ToString() == "System.Text");
}
```

The target file has a method that requires the using directives that
GenerateUsingDirectives() should generate.

Writing tests for refactorings is a good thing for the same reasons specified in the
"Unit Testing" section in Chapter 2, but we still need to test it in Visual Studio. We'll
briefly explore that in the next section.

VSIX Installation

In the "Executing the Refactoring" section, you saw how you can launch Visual Studio
with your refactoring installed. You can also run that separate instance of Visual Studio
under the debugger. We won't repeat that discussion again, just remember to run your
refactoring in Visual Studio before you deploy it. As you saw in the previous section, the
process by which you get a Document object can affect the results of the refactoring.

Also, the VSIX option is the only option you have to deploy and install your
refactorings to other users. There is no NuGet option provided with the default template.
This may change in the future, but for now extensions are the way to go to get your
refactorings to other developers.

■ **Note** For more information on adding NuGet support for refactorings, see
http://stackoverflow.com/questions/33118238/ship-roslyn-code-refactoring-as-
nuget-package.

We've covered testing your refactorings. Now it's now time to go through the
Workspaces API in more detail.

Interacting with a Workspace

With diagnostics and refactorings, we've touched upon the concept of a Workspace and its
related objects. In this section, we'll dive a little deeper and explore how they're laid out and
how you can use them to automatically update documents with projects and solutions.

What Is a Workspace?

Ever since .NET developers have been using Visual Studio, they've been accustomed to a
specific code layout. A simple example is any of the figures in this chapter that show the
Solution Explorer (like Figure 3-7). Each solution can contain one or more projects, and
each project can contain one or more documents. Solutions and projects can also have
zero subelements, but then they're kind of useless!

Given this typical structure, it was essential that the Compiler API have a similar object model in place. It's pretty rare for code to live in isolation—that is, you only have one file in a project and that's all you compile. Applications are complex combinations of projects, where changes in one piece of code can have significant ramifications. In the "Creating a Refactoring Solution" section earlier in this chapter, the Renamer.RenameSymbolAsync() was mentioned. That method needs a Solution object because it will look for the usage of a member (like a method) that has been renamed and change it for the developer wherever it's referenced in a solution. The Workspace API gives you an abstraction over this solution structure. Figure 3-15 gives a simplistic view of the Workspace object model.

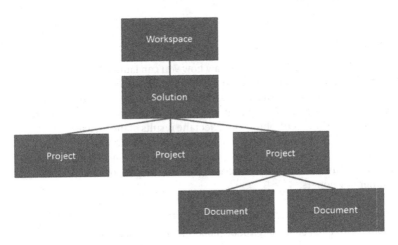

Figure 3-15. *Workspace object model*

A Workspace contains one Solution, referenced by the CurrentSolution property. Each Solution contains Project objects, and each Project has Document objects. The documents can be any file, whether it's a code, resource, or text file.

This model doesn't impose one specific implementation of the API. All of these classes are not sealed, so you can create your own version of a Workspace. There are three that you may see as you work with the Compiler API. Let's briefly investigate each of them in the next section.

■ **Note** The Workspace API may have members like the FilePath property on a Document, but that doesn't mean that an implementation of the Workspace API has to be file-based. You could create a custom Workspace object model that just used memory or a database for its persistence mechansim.

Common Workspace Implementations

The AdhocWorkspace, as its name suggests, is useful when you want to quickly create a Workspace and related objects. We've used them in our unit tests in both this chapter and Chapter 2. As a refresher, here's how you create a project from a Workspace's current Solution:

```
var projectName = "Test";
var projectId = ProjectId.CreateNewId(projectName);

var solution = new AdhocWorkspace().CurrentSolution;
var project = solution.AddProject(
  projectId, projectName, projectName, LanguageNames.CSharp);
```

Typically, AdhocWorkspace is only used in testing scenarios. You can find these types in the Microsoft.CodeAnalysis.Workspaces assembly.

The MSBuildWorkspace class is another implementation of the Workspace API. This workspace's name also implies its target: MSBuild. You'll use this workspace when you interact with an MSBuild process. You'll see this class in action in the "Using a Custom MSBuild Task for Automatic Updates" section later in this chapter. You can find this workspace in the Microsoft.CodeAnalysis.Workspaces.Desktop assembly.

Finally, the VisualStudioWorkspace class is the workspace you use when your analyzer or refactoring is running within Visual Studio. We'll use this workspace in the "Creating a Visual Studio Extension" section. This type exists in the Microsoft.VisualStudio.LanguageServices assembly.

■ **Note** If you look carefully, the actual type for the workspace you see in Visual Studio is Microsoft.VisualStudio.LanguageServices.RoslynVisualStudioWorkspace. That's a class that indirectly inherits from VisualStudioWorkspace, but it's a small detail that you shouldn't worry about.

You now know what Workspace implementations exist. In the next section, we'll use the last two—MSBuildWorkspace and VisualStudioWorkspace—to do some automation with our refactorings.

Updating Solutions and Projects

Refactorings are good to have because they assist a developer to create cleaner, more manageable code, but there's an area with refactorings that needs to be addressed. There are cases where I want my code to be updated such that features like code formatting are done automatically, without me having to perform any manual intervention. For example, there's an extension called Productivity Power Tools that executes some refactorings for you. Once you install it, you can configure it to remove and sort using directives along with formatting code when you save a file. Figure 3-16 shows that configuration screen.

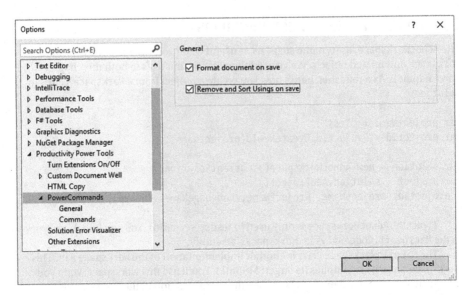

Figure 3-16. *Using Productivity Power Tools to automatically apply formatting and using directive cleanup*

■ **Note** To learn more about using Productivity Power Tools, see
`https://visualstudiogallery.msdn.microsoft.com/34ebc6a2-2777-421d-8914-e29c1dfa7f5d`.

Unfortunately, the refactoring template gives developers a somewhat restricted view on Visual Studio integration. Thankfully, we're not limited by that template. We'll go through two techniques to allow your refactorings to be automatically applied in a solution. But before we do that, let's come up with a simple refactoring that you may (or may not!) like: removing comments.

■ **Note** In the upcoming Visual Studio 15 preview (the next version after Visual Studio 2015), there's a prototype of a feature that may allow developers to create "styling" analyzers that will automatically be enforced by Visual Studio. It's a work in progress; visit the following link (and check out the "Custom Code Style Enforcement" section) for more details: `https://blogs.msdn.microsoft.com/dotnet/2016/04/02/whats-new-for-c-and-vb-in-visual-studio/`.

Creating the CommentRemover Refactoring

We'll create a refactoring that removes any comments within a given syntax node. Keep in mind, this is just an example. It's not a suggestion that comments are bad in any way. I try to keep comments to a bare minimum, but there are cases where a comment can help others figure out why code is the way it is. Use this refactoring carefully—if you force it upon your teammates, the response may not be positive! But it is a simple refactoring in the sense that comments do not affect a compilation result, so removing them is a fairly trivial endeavour.

We have to be careful of one thing, though, and that's what comments we remove. Take a look at the following code:

```
public class Commentary
{
    /// <summary>
    /// Adds commentary to a piece of text.
    /// </summary>
    /// <param name="text">The text to process.</param>
    public void Process(string text)
    {
        // Here's where the real work goes.

        /*
        Maybe more work goes here.
        */
    }
}
```

We definitely want to keep XML comments. Those show up in Intellisense and can assist developers as they write their code. The single- and multiline comments like the ones within Process() are the ones that we want to get rid of. How are these represented in the Compiler API?

All of the comments are represented by a SyntaxTrivia struct. The multiline comment has the Kind property equal to SyntaxKind.MultiLineCommentTrivia. The single-line comment's Kind property is SyntaxKind.SingleLineCommentTrivia. Finally, the XML comments have a Kind of SyntaxKind.SingleLineDocumentationCommentTrivia. Therefore, all we'll need to do is find trivia elements with the right Kind value, and replace those with empty nodes. Let's create an extension that will do just that to any SyntaxNode it gets.

For this solution, which we'll call CommentRemover; we won't use the refactoring template. We'll create a class library that references the Compiler API, and then we'll have one extension method that performs the necessary comment cleansing. In subsequent chapter sections we'll reuse that extension method to provide automatic comment removal. Listing 3-9 shows how that extension method works.

Listing 3-9. Removing comments from a given SyntaxNode

```
public static class SyntaxNodeExtensions
{
  public static T RemoveComments<T>(this T @this)
    where T : SyntaxNode
  {
    var triviaToRemove = new List<SyntaxTrivia>();

    var nodesWithComments = @this.DescendantNodesAndTokens(_ => true)
      .Where(_ => _.HasLeadingTrivia &&
        _.GetLeadingTrivia().Any(__ =>
          __.IsKind(SyntaxKind.SingleLineCommentTrivia) ||
          __.IsKind(SyntaxKind.MultiLineCommentTrivia)));

    var commentCount = 0;

    foreach (var nodeWithComments in nodesWithComments)
    {
      var leadingTrivia = nodeWithComments.GetLeadingTrivia();

      for (var i = 0; i < leadingTrivia.Count; i++)
      {
        var trivia = leadingTrivia[i];
        if (trivia.IsKind(SyntaxKind.SingleLineCommentTrivia) ||
          trivia.IsKind(SyntaxKind.MultiLineCommentTrivia))
        {
          triviaToRemove.Add(trivia);
          commentCount++;

          if (i > 0)
          {
            var precedingTrivia = leadingTrivia[i - 1];

            if (precedingTrivia.IsKind(SyntaxKind.WhitespaceTrivia))
            {
              triviaToRemove.Add(precedingTrivia);
            }
          }
        }
      }
    }

    triviaToRemove.AddRange(leadingTrivia.Where(_ =>
      _.IsKind(SyntaxKind.EndOfLineTrivia))
      .Take(commentCount));
  }
```

```
    return triviaToRemove.Count > 0 ?
      @this.ReplaceTrivia(
        triviaToRemove, (_, _) => new SyntaxTrivia())
      .WithAdditionalAnnotations(Formatter.Annotation) :
      @this;
  }
}
```

We find all of the nodes and tokens that have leading trivia that contains single- or multi-line comments. Then we go through the trivia list and add comment trivia to our list. If the comments begin with any whitespace, we add those to our list. We also remove any end of line trivia for the comment lines. Finally, we remove all the identified trivia from the current node if we found any trivia to remove. This code may seem a little awkward, but it's done this way to keep the formatting of the developer's code consistent—that is, we don't want to leave empty lines in the code when we remove the comment trivia.

Now that we have an extension method to remove comments from a SytnaxNode instance, let's see where we can use it such that it's done automatically for the developer. Our first option is to use a console application, which we'll implement in the next section.

Using the Command Line for Automatic Updates

One of the extension points in a project is to invoke pre- and post-build events. Figure 3-17 shows what this looks like in the project's Properties tab.

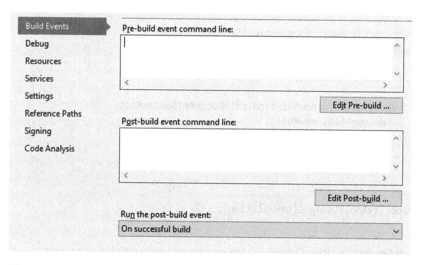

Figure 3-17. Project build event properties

Anything that can be run from the command line can be done in the two text boxes shown in Figure 3-17. Therefore, what we can do is create a console application that will get the file location of a project or solution, and then invoke RemoveComment() on every file's CompilationUnitSytnax node.

To do this, we need to provide a couple of helper methods in CommentRemover— RemoveCommentsFromSolutionAsync() and RemoveCommentsFromProjectAsync()–to use the Workspace API. We'll go through RemoveCommentsFromSolutionAsync() in the book. The other helper method, RemoveCommentsFromProjectAsync(), is virtually identical except it starts with a Project object, not a Solution:

```
public static async Task RemoveCommentsFromSolutionAsync(
  string solutionFile)
{
  var workspace = MSBuildWorkspace.Create();
  var solution = await workspace.OpenSolutionAsync(solutionFile);
  var newSolution = solution;

  foreach (var projectId in solution.ProjectIds)
  {
    var project = newSolution.GetProject(projectId);

    foreach (var documentId in project.DocumentIds)
    {
      var document = newSolution.GetDocument(documentId);

      if (Path.GetExtension(document.FilePath).ToLower() == ".cs")
      {
        var root = await document.GetSyntaxRootAsync();
        var newRoot = root.RemoveComments();

        if (root != newRoot)
        {
          newSolution = newSolution.WithDocumentSyntaxRoot(
            documentId, newRoot);
        }
      }
    }
  }

  workspace.TryApplyChanges(newSolution);
}
```

We call Create() on MSBuildWorkspace to get a workspace, which we can use to open a solution file. From that solution, we go through each project and its documents. If we find a C# file, we update that document if RemoveComments() produced any changes. Once we've navigated each file, we call TryApplyChanges() to commit any changes to the solution and its members.

The other part of this solution is to create a console application project that references the CommentRemover class library project. It also needs the Compiler API assemblies from NuGet. Once those are in place, here's what Main() does:

```
static void Main(string[] args)
{
  //System.Diagnostics.Debugger.Launch();

  if (args.Length == 0 || args[0] == string.Empty)
  {
    Console.Out.WriteLine(
      "Usage: CommentRemover.ConsoleApplication {solution or project
      file}");
  }

  var file = args[0];

  if (!File.Exists(file))
  {
    Console.Out.WriteLine($"File {file} does not exist.");
  }
  else
  {
    if (Path.GetExtension(file) == ".sln")
    {
      WorkspaceCommentRemover.RemoveCommentsFromSolutionAsync(file).Wait();
    }
    else if (Path.GetExtension(file) == ".csproj")
    {
      WorkspaceCommentRemover.RemoveCommentsFromProjectAsync(file).Wait();
    }
    else
    {
      Console.Out.WriteLine("Only .sln and .csproj files are supported.");
    }
  }
}
```

Most of this code is just data validation to ensure that we have a file path in the args array that we can give to one of the WorkspaceCommentRemover helper methods.

With the console application in place, we now need to update its postbuild command so that it pushes its build content to a common directory:

```
xcopy "$(TargetDir)*.*" "$(SolutionDir)ConsoleApplicationOutput\*.*" /Y /E /C
```

Now we can create a test project that will execute this application on its prebuild event:

```
"$(SolutionDir)ConsoleApplicationOutput\CommentRemover.ConsoleApplication.exe"
"$(ProjectPath)"
```

We need to make sure that this test integration project doesn't build before the console application is built. To do this without having an explicit reference to the console application, we can tell the solution in Visual Studio about this build dependency. Right-click on the solution and select Project Dependencies. Figure 3-18 shows how to set this dependency correctly.

Figure 3-18. *Setting explicit project dependencies in a solution*

With this configuration in place, a project's code (like CommentRemover. ConsoleApplication.IntegrationTests) will get every comment removed when it's built. That's something that can't be visualized in a picture, but Figure 3-19 shows the integration project with a C# file open when the console application is done with its comment removal.

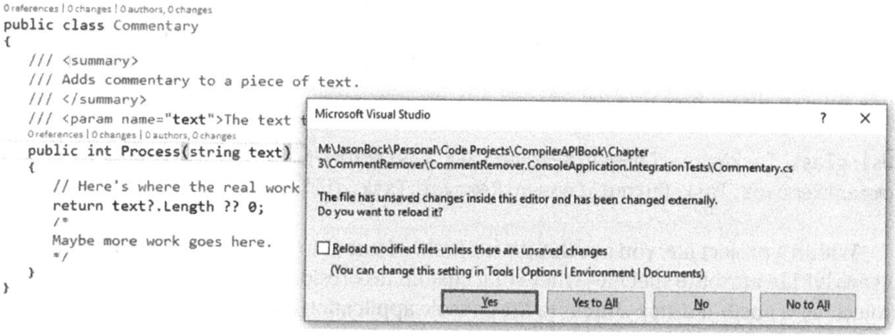

Figure 3-19. *Evidence that the console application has made changes*

Because the file has been updated, Visual Studio will ask if you want to see those changes. When you click Yes, you'll see the code with all the comments removed, except the XML comments.

Another way to automatically run code during a build process is to use a custom MSBuild task. Let's look at that technique in the next section.

Using a Custom MSBuild Task for Automatic Updates

An MSBuild process is essentially a number of tasks executed to compile code, move files into other directories, and so on. You can customize this process by defining your own tasks and including them into a project file. To do this, you create a class library and reference the Microsoft.Build.Framework and Microsoft.Build.Utilities.Core assemblies (along with the Compiler API Nuget packages). Then you can create your custom task by defining a class that inherits from the Task class, as shown in Listing 3-10.

Listing 3-10. Defining a custom MSBuild task

```
public class CommentRemoverTask
  : MBU.Task
{
  public override bool Execute()
  {
    WorkspaceCommentRemover.RemoveCommentsFromProjectAsync(
      this.ProjectFilePath).Wait();
    return true;
  }

  [Required]
  public string ProjectFilePath { get; set; }
}
```

Because most of the work is done in RemoveCommentsFromProjectAsync(), the implementation of the custom Task is thin. The only member we need to add is ProjectFilePath, which we'll use when we invoke this task in a project file. The following code snippet shows how that works:

```
<UsingTask TaskName="CommentRemoverTask" AssemblyFile="$(SolutionDir)
CommentRemover.Task Output\CommentRemover.Task.dll" />
```

Within a project file, you use the <UsingTask> element to give the task a name. The AssemblyFile attribute specifies where that custom task resides. The CommentRemover.Task project has a postbuild step similar to the console application, where it will copy all of its output to a directory. That directory is what AssemblyFile uses.

To invoke the task, you can include it within either the BeforeBuild or AfterBuild tasks; remember to set the ProjectFilePath property correctly:

```
<Target Name="AfterBuild">
  <CommentRemoverTask ProjectFilePath="$(ProjectPath)" />
</Target>
```

The next time the project is built, all the comments in any C# file will be removed.

With both the console application and custom MSBuild Task approaches, we used the MSBuildWorkspace to modify document content within projects. In the next section, we'll create a Visual Studio extension that will use VisualStudioWorkspace.

Creating a Visual Studio Extension

Although both of the previous techniques worked (creating a command-line tool and a custom MSBuild task), they require manual intervention to ensure they were integrated correctly. When you're updating project files and creating post-build steps, it's not hard to do something wrong during the setup. Another option is creating extensions for Visual Studio. The advantage of this approach is the developer just double-clicks on a VSIX file or goes to the Visual Studio Gallery to find and install it. As an extension author, you have the ability to extend pretty much every aspect of Visual Studio. However, writing extensions is not a trivial endeavor. We won't go through all of the options available to you when you create extensions, but let's create a simple one that will provide that automatic comment removal behavior.

■ **Note** If you want more information about extending Visual Studio, please check out the reference at https://msdn.microsoft.com/en-us/library/dn919654.aspx.

To create the project, you'll go into the Extensibility node when you add a new project, and select "VSIX Project" as shown in Figure 3-20.

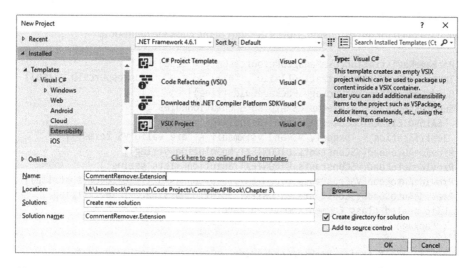

Figure 3-20. *Creating an extension project*

Note If you don't see the VSIX Project option, you'll need to install the Visual Studio SDK. You can get more information about the SDK at `https://msdn.microsoft.com/en-us/library/bb166441.aspx`.

Next, we need to get a package class file in this project. Add a "Visual Studio Package" file to the project, as shown in Figure 3-21.

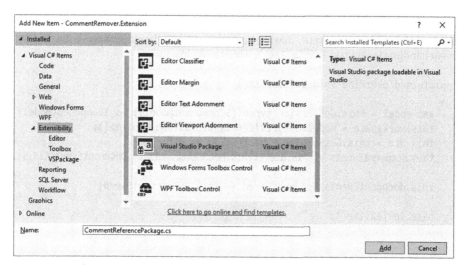

Figure 3-21. *Adding a package file to the extension project*

You can leave the file as-is; I modified it a bit to get rid of some noise and focus on what we need for our extension. Here's the start of the class file definition:

```
[PackageRegistration(UseManagedResourcesOnly = true)]
[InstalledProductRegistration("#110", "#112", "1.0", IconResourceID = 400)]
[Guid(CommentRemoverPackage.PackageGuidString)]
[SuppressMessage("StyleCop.CSharp.DocumentationRules",
  "SA1650:ElementDocumentationMustBeSpelledCorrectly",
  Justification = "pkgdef, VS and vsixmanifest are valid VS terms")]
[ProvideAutoLoad(VSConstants.UICONTEXT.NoSolution_string)]
[ProvideAutoLoad(VSConstants.UICONTEXT.SolutionExists_string)]
[ProvideAutoLoad(VSConstants.UICONTEXT.SolutionHasMultipleProjects_string)]
[ProvideAutoLoad(VSConstants.UICONTEXT.SolutionHasSingleProject_string)]
public sealed class CommentRemoverPackage
  : Package
{
  public const string PackageGuidString = "7e923ca1-8495-48f9-a429-
0373e32500d1";

  private DTE dte;
  private DocumentEventsClass documentEvents;
  private VisualStudioWorkspace workspace;
```

The first four class attributes along with `PackageGuidString` were created by the file template. They're important for Visual Studio to use our package correctly but we don't need to be concerned about their details now. The `ProvideAutoLoad` attributes (which are not generated by default) are important, because our package needs to be loaded and ready to go as soon as Visual Studio starts. We don't want to wait for a developer to open a tool window for our package's implementation to be alive. These attributes inform Visual Studio to initilize our package when Visual Studio is launched. The private fields are needed so we can react to events that are happening when a developer saves a file. That event handling is set up in `Initialize()`, which looks like this:

```
protected override void Initialize()
{
  var model = this.GetService(typeof(SComponentModel)) as IComponentModel;
  this.workspace = model.GetService<VisualStudioWorkspace>();
  this.dte = this.GetService(typeof(DTE)) as DTE;
  this.documentEvents = this.dte.Events.DocumentEvents as DocumentEventsClass;

  this.documentEvents.DocumentSaved += this.OnDocumentSaved;

  base.Initialize();
}
```

```
protected override void Dispose(bool disposing)
{
  this.documentEvents.DocumentSaved -= this.OnDocumentSaved;
  base.Dispose(disposing);
}
```

We need to get a reference to the VisualStudioWorkspace and DTE (design time enviroment) objects, which we can get via GetService(). Once we have them, we set up an event handler to listen for documents that are saved. We also override Dispose() to remove the event handler. Listing 3-11 shows what OnDocumentSaved() does.

Listing 3-11. Implementing the DocumentSaved event in a Visual Studio extension

```
private void OnDocumentSaved(EnvDTE.Document dteDocument)
{
  var documentIds = this.workspace.CurrentSolution
    .GetDocumentIdsWithFilePath(dteDocument.FullName);

  if(documentIds != null && documentIds.Length == 1)
  {
    var documentId = documentIds[0];
    var document = this.workspace.CurrentSolution.GetDocument(documentId);

    if (Path.GetExtension(document.FilePath) == ".cs")
    {
      SyntaxNode root = null;

      if (document.TryGetSyntaxRoot(out root))
      {
        var newRoot = root.RemoveComments();

        if (newRoot != root)
        {
          var newSolution = document.Project.Solution
            .WithDocumentSyntaxRoot(document.Id, newRoot);
          this.workspace.TryApplyChanges(newSolution);
          dteDocument.Save();
        }
      }
    }
  }
}
```

We need to bridge the DTE and VisualStudioWorkspace worlds to figure out the document's identifier. We can do this by using GetDocumentIdsWithFilePath(). If we find the identifier, we use it to get a Document instance via GetDocument(). If we end up changing the root node of the document by removing all the comments, we apply those changes to the solution. We also need to invoke Save() on the DTEDocument instance. If we don't do this, the changes will show up in Visual Studio, but the document will be in an edited state again. Calling Save() ensures that the changes are saved to disk.

Just like the VSIX projects for analyzers and refactorings, if you make the project the startup project for the solution, Visual Studio will launch another instance of Visual Studio with your extension automatically installed. It's hard to demonstrate in static text this package in action, so I encourage you to download the code and try it out yourself. Create a project, add a C# file and put comments in the code. As soon as you save the file, your comments will be removed.

One last point about the VSIX project that is generated. By default, the package is strong-named, so any assemblies that it uses must be strong-named as well. Our CommentRemover class library isn't, so if we don't make changes to the extension project, we'll get exceptions like FileNotFoundException, informing us that strong-named code can't call code from assemblies that aren't strong names. You can turn strong-naming off in the extension project from the Signing tab of the project's Properties view, as shown in Figure 3-22.

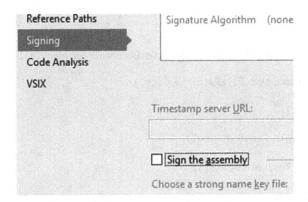

Figure 3-22. *Turning off assembly strong-naming*

Conclusion

In this chapter, you learned to create your own refactorings to help developers improve code using the Compiler API. You also used the Workspace API in a number of scenarios to implement automatic refactorings throughout a solution. In the next chapter, we'll explore the Scripting API.

CHAPTER 4

Using the Scripting API

So far, all the C# code you've seen hasn't been any different from what you've been able to do in C# since version 1.0. That is, you still write C# code, you compile it, and an assembly is generated. Although having the inner workings of the compiler available for public consumption via the Compiler API empowers developers to analyze and transform their code, nothing has substantially altered the flow of the compilation process. However, that changes with the Update 1 release of Visual Studio 2015, because within the Compiler API is a brand-new Scripting API. With the Scripting API, C# can be treated as a scripting language. In this chapter, I'll show you how to use the Scripting API to provide a dynamic way to augment applications. But before we do that, let me briefly define what a scripting language really is.

What Is a Scripting Language?

Before we get into the details of the Scripting API, let's spend some time on scripting languages in general. What makes a language a "scripting" language? What are its characteristics? How does it work? Are scripting languages substantially different from other languages? Knowing the realm that you're entering in this chapter will help you understand the Scripting API better and how C# fits in the domain of scripting languages.

Orchestrating an Environment

Traditionally, scripting languages have been viewed as "glue" languages. They're usually not as powerful as other popular programming languages if their feature sets are compared and contrasted. However, their power lies in their simplicity. They're not designed to build complex domain layers or implement web servers; rather, they work with a given system and extend it in ways that the original designers may not have intended. They'll tie different parts and members together to create new functionality without having to go through a typical compile, test, and deploy scenario that most applications will partake in. Essentially, they *orchestrate* different pieces available to them.

Well-known scripting languages that developers have used are Bash, Python, and Lua. Another that developers in the .NET arena may have heard of and used in their applications is Visual Basic for Applications (VBA). VBA allows developers to control Office applications in a programmic way. The object model for an Office application may seem quite complex at first, but you can record macros in an Office application to see the pieces of the object model in action. Figure 4-1 shows the VBA macro editor with a snippet of code that was created by me just typing into Word.

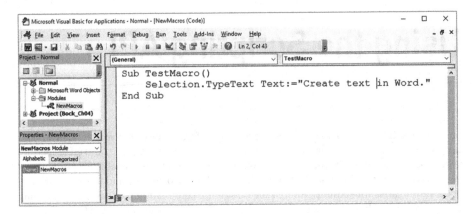

Figure 4-1. *Creating macros in Word*

By using the Macros ➤ Record Macros feature in Word (which is on the View menu), I was able to figure out that by using TypeText on the Selection object, I could insert whatever text I wanted to. Of course, there are far more objects and methods available to you to control whatever part of Word you want to, but you don't have to remember every one. All you have to do is record your interaction and let Word generate the code for you.

Dynamic Capabilities

Another common aspect of a scripting language is its dynamic nature. Dynamic languages are those where the notion of types is a loose, or even nonexistent, one. Types can also be changed as the code executes. Examples of languages like this are Ruby and JavaScript. These languages have the notion of classes, but class definitions can change dramatically as code executes. Keep in mind that a scripting language can also be statically typed. There's no hard-and-fast rule when it comes to the dynamic capabilities of a language and whether that qualifies it as a scripting language.

In essence, any language can be considered a scripting language if an environment exists to provide the user with a dynamic experience. This is typically done with something called a Read, Evaluate, Print, Loop (REPL). Developers will use a REPL to try different ways to run their scripts and to immediately execute functionality available to the REPL. Lots of languages have this capability, but C# has always lacked this within the APIs provided by the .NET Framework. However, now with the Scripting API, you can treat C# as a scripting language. Let's start our investigation of the Scripting API by looking at a tool that uses this API in Visual Studio: the C# REPL.

Using the C# REPL

Shipping with Update 1 of Visual Studio 2015 is the C# Interactive window. It's a REPL that uses the Scripting API to allow developers to quickly experiment with snippets of C#. You won't see Scripting API usage just yet in this section, but keep in mind that this Visual Studio feature is powered by the Scripting API. By seeing how this window works, you'll better understand the capabilities available in the Scripting API to power dynamic programming experiences.

To start working with the C# Interactive window, open Visual Studio, and go to View ➤ Other Windows ➤ C# Interactive window. Note that you don't have to open or create a project to start working with this window. Type "3 + 5" in the window and press the Enter key. Figure 4-2 shows what you should see.

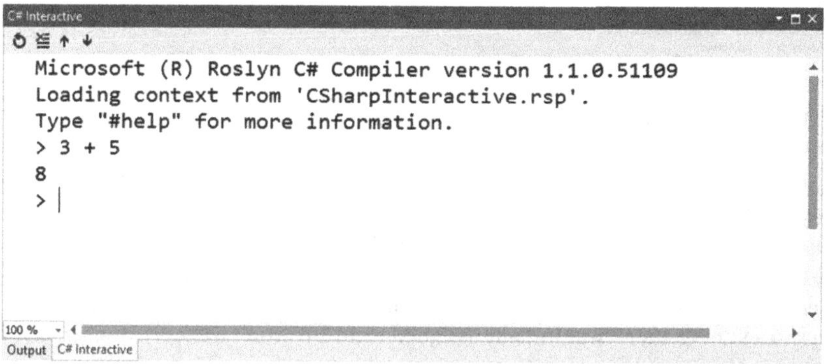

Figure 4-2. Performing simple calculations within the C# Interactive window

As a developer would expect, executing simple arithmetic calculations works. Let's set the value of that calculation to a variable called x. Once we do that, we can print out its value, as shown in Figure 4-3.

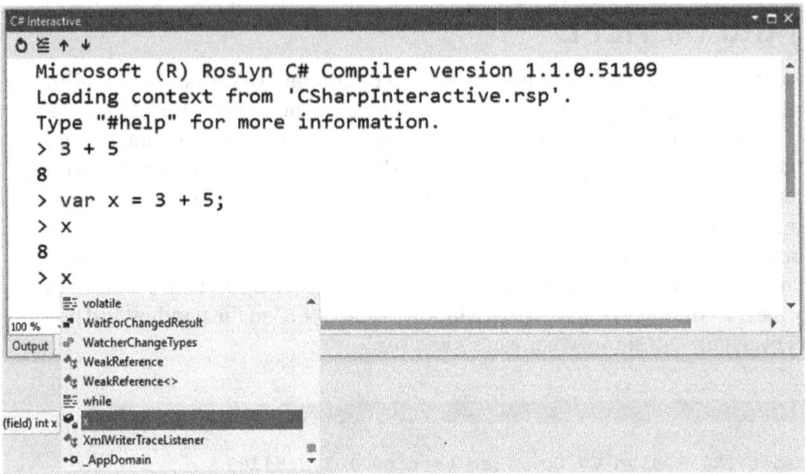

Figure 4-3. *Printing the value of a variable*

What's interesting to note in Figure 4-3 is that you get Intellisense within the interactive window. It knows there's a variable called x within the scope of this interactive session. It also knows that the variable is typed as an int. Scripting languages have a tendency to have very loose typing semantics, but even though the Interactive window is a scripting environment, C# retains its strong typing semantic. Figure 4-4 shows that assigning x to a string after it was initially assigned to an int won't work.

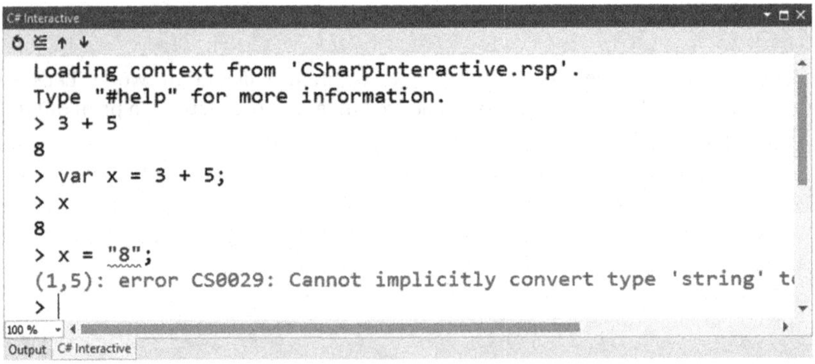

Figure 4-4. *Strong typing in the C# Interactive window*

At any time in the window you can type #help to learn different commands that are available during the session. A sample of the #help output is shown in Figure 4-5.

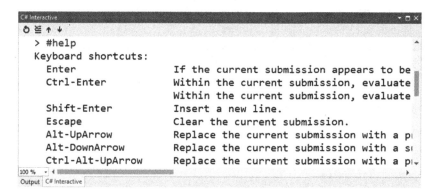

Figure 4-5. *Using help to display various commands*

For example, you can type #cls to clear the screen. You can also use #reset to clear any current script state. Figure 4-6 shows what happens after you type #reset and then look at the value for x.

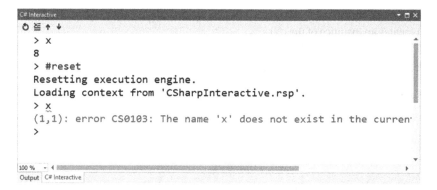

Figure 4-6. *Resetting the interactive session*

You can also define types within the session. To do this, you start typing the definition of a class, and then press Enter. The Interactive window will go into a multiline edit mode, so you can add members to the class, like fields, properties, and constructors. Figure 4-7 shows what the window looks like when you define a class.

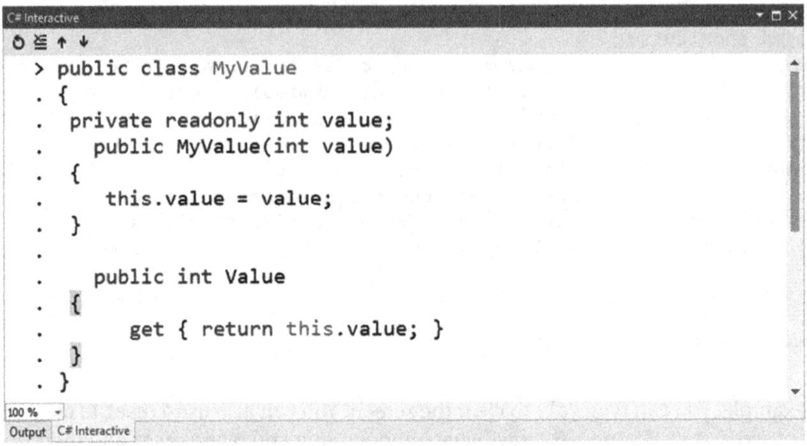

Figure 4-7. *Creating a class in the Interactive window*

Once the class is defined, you can use it in your session. Figure 4-8 demonstrates code that creates an instance of the class.

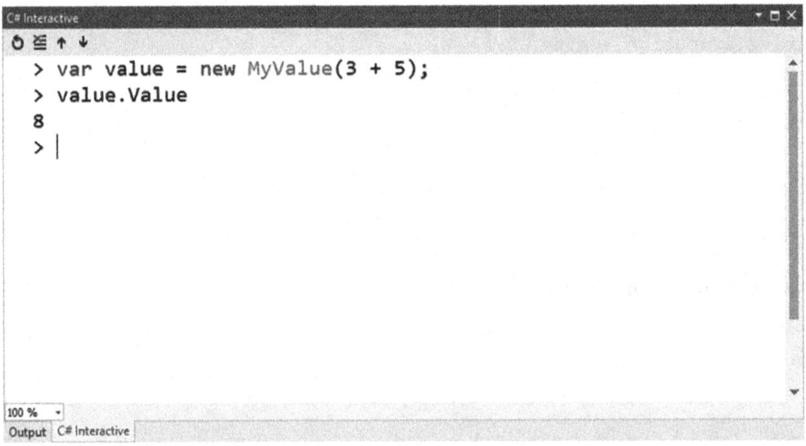

Figure 4-8. *Using classes defined in the Interactive window*

Note that the Interactive window experience isn't limited to Visual Studio. If you bring up the Developer Command Prompt for VS2015 (from the Windows Start menu), you can type "csi" and get the same experience from a command window (without Intellisense). Figure 4-9 shows what that looks like.

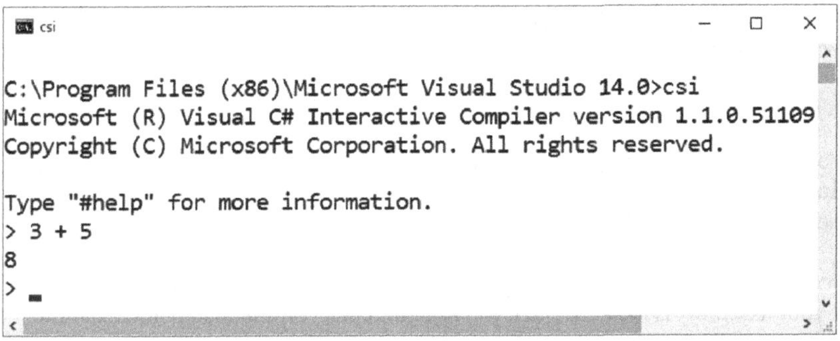

Figure 4-9. *Getting an interactive C# experience from the command line*

That's the basics of the Interactive window in Visual Studio. Now let's look at how to use code assets within the Interactive window.

Loading Code in Script

Creating code in the Interactive window is a great way to try different implementations without needing to create a Visual Studio solution. However, you may want to load references to other assemblies or previous code snippets in the Interactive window. Let's tackle the assembly loading issue first. To do this, you use the #r directive, which requires a full path to the location of the assembly file. Once its loaded, you can reference types from that assembly as you normally would. You can even include using statements in your session.

To see assembly referencing in action, create a Class Library project in Visual Studio. Add one class called MyValue that is structured the same way as the code in Figure 4-7 earlier in the chapter. After you've compiled the code, figure out the path where the assembly file exists. When you know where that is, you can type in the code you see in Figure 4-10 (notice that your path will be different than the one shown in the figure).

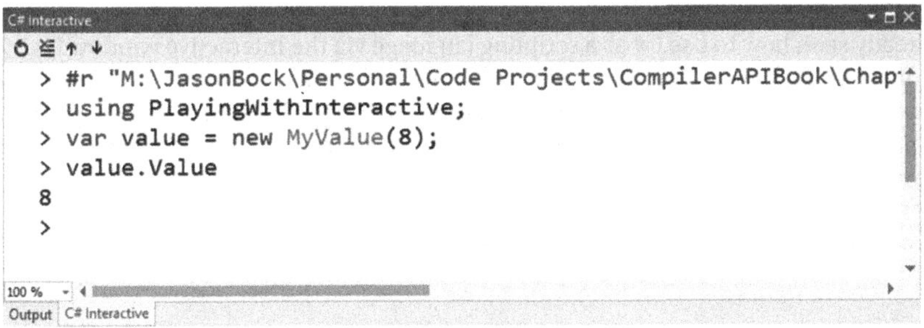

Figure 4-10. *Loading assemblies within the Interactive window*

After the assembly is loaded, you can reference namespaces within that assembly via the using statement.

At this point, there is no easy way to save all the code entered in the session to a file. The only way to do this is to manually navigate to every line in the session buffer via the Alt + Arrow Up keystroke and then copy each line of code to a text file. But once you have your code in a file, you can load it at any time via the #load directive. Let's say you captured code in Listing 4-1 to a text file.

Listing 4-1. Creating a simple C# script file

```
#r "C:\YourCodePath\PlayingWithInteractive.dll"
using PlayingWithInteractive;
var value = new MyValue(8);
```

Notice that the path to load the assembly in Listing 4-1 would have to change based on where your assembly is located. Once you have that file, you can load it and examine variables that were created from the script, as shown in Figure 4-11.

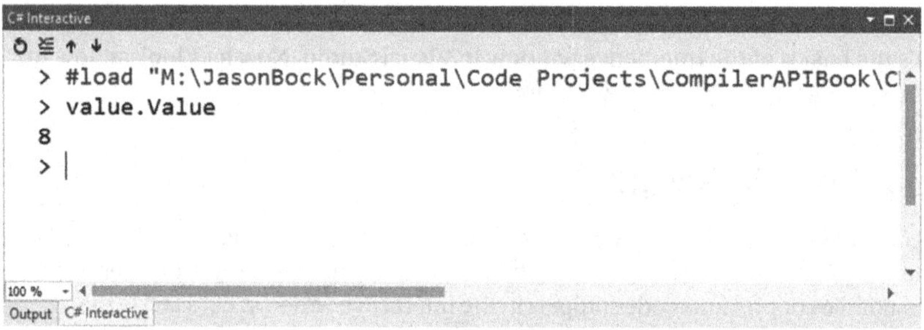

Figure 4-11. *Loading C# script in the Interactive window*

At this point, you should have a good understanding of how the Interactive window works in Visual Studio. Let's move our focus away from the Interactive window and direct it toward the code that powers its implementation: the Scripting API.

Making C# Interactive

You've already seen how to use C# as a scripting language via the Interactive window in Visual Studio and the csi.exe command line tool. Now we'll look at the Scripting API so you can use it to create extensible applications within .NET. You'll execute C# code as it's entered, preserve state from script execution to script execution, and even analyze the structure of C# script code.

Referencing the Scripting NuGet Package

The first activity you need to do is get the right NuGet package installed into your project. This is pretty simple to do. Let's say you create a simple console application called ScriptingPlayground. All you need to do is reference the Microsoft.CodeAnalysis. Scripting package, as shown in Figure 4-12.

Figure 4-12. *Referencing the NuGet package for the Scripting API*

Once NuGet is done, you should see two referenced assemblies with "Scripting" in their name, as shown in Figure 4-13.

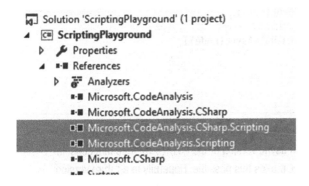

Figure 4-13. *Scripting API assemblies referenced in a project*

Now that the project has the right references in place, let's start using members from the Scripting API.

Evaluating Scripts

The main class you'll use for scripting is called CSharpScript. Its API surface is pretty small, meaning that it doesn't have a lot of methods, but within those methods is all of the power to make C# scriptable. Let's start by creating a simple class that will evaluate any code given to it in a console window. This is shown in Listing 4-2.

Listing 4-2. Evaluating code via EvalulateAsync()

```
using Microsoft.CodeAnalysis.CSharp.Scripting;
using Nito.AsyncEx;
using System;
using System.Threading.Tasks;

namespace ScriptingPlayground
{
  class Program
  {
    static void Main(string[] args)
    {
      AsyncContext.Run(() => Program.MainAsync(args));
    }

    private static async Task MainAsync(string[] args)
    {
      await Program.EvaluateCodeAsync();
    }

    private static async Task EvaluateCodeAsync()
    {
      Console.Out.WriteLine("Enter in your script:");
      var code = Console.In.ReadLine();
      Console.Out.WriteLine
        (await CSharpScript.EvaluateAsync(code));
    }
  }
}
```

■ **Note** The `AsyncContext` class comes from a NuGet package called Nito.AsyncEx. Currently in .NET you can't create an async version of the `Main()` method in a console application. But using `AsyncContext` makes this possible. Hopefully in a future version of .NET console applications will have this capability without needing a helper class. It's currently a feature request on the Roslyn GitHub site (`https://github.com/dotnet/roslyn/ issues/1695`), but it's unclear if it will be included in a future C# release.

Executing code via CSharpScript is as simple as calling EvaluateAsync(). Figure 4-14 shows what the console window looks like when the application evaluates code.

Figure 4-14. Evaluating code via the Scripting API

If you pass code that contains errors to EvaluateAsync(), you'll get a CompilationErrorException. This exception has a Diagnostics property on it that you can use to identify what the errors are with the code that was evaluated.

Although EvaluateAsync() lets you run simple pieces of C# code, there's more that you can do with scripting than just code evaluation. You can allow the script to use types and members for other assemblies. For example, let's say you created this class in an assembly called ScriptingContext:

```
public sealed class Context
{
  public Context(int value)
  {
    this.Value = value;
  }

  public int Value { get; }
}
```

Assuming that your console application has a reference to the ScriptingContext assembly, you can allow script code to use the Context class by passing a ScriptOptions object to EvaluateAsync(). Listing 4-3 shows how this works.

Listing 4-3. Passing in assembly references to script evaluation

```
private static async Task EvaluateCodeWithContextAsync()
{
  Console.Out.WriteLine("Enter in your script:");
  var code = Console.In.ReadLine();
  Console.Out.WriteLine(
    await CSharpScript.EvaluateAsync(code,
      options: ScriptOptions.Default
        .AddReferences(typeof(Context).Assembly)
        .AddImports(typeof(Context).Namespace)));
}
```

117

All you need to do is add a reference to the assembly that houses the Context class via AddReferences(). The AddImports() call essentially adds a using statement with the namespace of the Context class to the script context. Therefore, a developer doesn't have to provide the full type name of the class. Once you change the console application to call EvaluateCodeWithContextAsync() on startup, you can reference the Context class in your script. Figure 4-15 shows what this looks like.

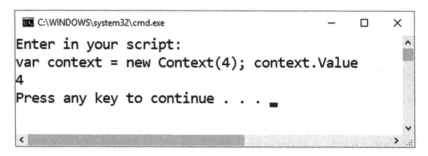

Figure 4-15. *Using custom types in script*

As you can see in Figure 4-15, the code can use the Context class without any issues.

You can also provide an instance of an object to the script, allowing the script to use members on that object. For example, you can create a class called CustomContext that exposes a Context object and a TextWriter:

```
using System.IO;

namespace ScriptingContext
{
  public class CustomContext
  {
    public CustomContext(Context context, TextWriter myOut)
    {
      this.Context = context;
      this.MyOut = myOut;
    }

    public Context Context { get; }
    public TextWriter MyOut { get; }
  }
}
```

Then you can create an instance of CustomContext and set the globals argument to EvaluateAsync() to that CustomContext instance, as shown in Listing 4-4.

Listing 4-4. Using a global context object

```
private static async Task EvaluateCodeWithGlobalContextAsync()
{
  Console.Out.WriteLine("Enter in your script:");
  var code = Console.In.ReadLine();
  Console.Out.WriteLine(
    await CSharpScript.EvaluateAsync(code,
      globals: new CustomContext(
        new Context(4), Console.Out)));
}
```

Note that the Out property of the Console class is given to the CustomContext instance, letting the script print out information to the context. Figure 4-16 shows how you can use a script to print the Value property of the Context instance to the console window if you call EvaluateCodeWithGlobalContextAsync() from the async Main() method.

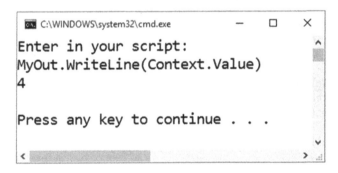

Figure 4-16. Using a global object in a script

So far, you've seen how to use EvaluateAsync() to immediately execute a piece of valid C# code. In the next section, I'll discuss how you can analyze the script before you execute it.

Analyzing Scripts

Running code via EvaluateAsync() requires a bit more care than what I've shown so far. For example, if there's syntax errors, you'll get a CompilationErrorException. Rather than adding an exception handler to code, you can use Create() on the CSharpScript class to be a bit more defensive in your script execution implementation. Furthermore, these methods expose syntax trees and semantic models, so you can query the submitted script for details on what it intends to do. Listing 4-5 demonstrates how you can perform this script analysis (note: assume this method is part of the Program class defined in the "Evaluating Scripts" section).

Listing 4-5. Analyzing a script's content

```
private static async Task CompileScriptAsync()
{
  Console.Out.WriteLine("Enter in your script:");
  var code = Console.In.ReadLine();
  var script = CSharpScript.Create(code);
  var compilation = script.GetCompilation();
  var diagnostics = compilation.GetDiagnostics();

  if(diagnostics.Length > 0)
  {
    foreach (var diagnostic in diagnostics)
    {
      Console.Out.WriteLine(diagnostic);
    }
  }
  else
  {
    foreach (var tree in compilation.SyntaxTrees)
    {
      var model = compilation.GetSemanticModel(tree);
      foreach (var node in tree.GetRoot().DescendantNodes(
        _ => true))
      {
        var symbol = model.GetSymbolInfo(node).Symbol;
        Console.Out.WriteLine(
          $"{node.GetType().Name} {node.GetText().ToString()}");

        if (symbol != null)
        {
          var symbolKind = Enum.GetName(
            typeof(SymbolKind), symbol.Kind);
          Console.Out.WriteLine(
            $"\t{symbolKind} {symbol.Name}");
        }
      }
    }

    Console.Out.WriteLine((await script.RunAsync()).ReturnValue);
  }
}
```

The return value of Create() is based on a Script<T> type, with T specified as an object (there's also a generic version of Create() you can use if you know what the script's return value will be in advance). From this Script<T> class, you can get compilation information with GetCompilation(), which returns a Compilation object. The Compilation class is the base class for the CSharpCompilation class you saw in

Chapter 1 in Listing 1-1. Therefore, you can look at diagnostic information, syntax trees, semantic models—everything that you learned about in Chapter 1 can be reused here to query the structure of the given script. In this example, if we have diagnostic information, we don't run the script; instead, we print out the error information. Otherwise, we display syntax and semantic information, and then run the script via RunAsync().

Let's see what the code in Listing 4-5 does with a valid script. Figure 4-17 shows the results of a successful script analysis.

Figure 4-17. *Analyzing a valid script*

Figure 4-18 shows what happens when the submitted script contains errors.

```
C:\WINDOWS\system32\cmd.exe                                  —    □    ×
Enter in your script:
var x = Syste.Guid.NewGuid(); x
(1,9): error CS0103: The name 'Syste' does not exist in the current context
Press any key to continue . . .
```

Figure 4-18. *Analyzing an invalid script*

There's one more aspect to scripts that I should mention: storing state. Let's look at how state works with scripts in the next section.

State Management in Scripts

So far the script examples within the "Making C# Interactive" section have all been done via a single execution of script. That is, we get a line of code from the user, execute that script, and then the program is done. As you saw with the C# REPL in the "Using the C# REPL" section, you can type numerous lines of script code and refer to variables and classes issued earlier in the code. Fortunately, we don't have to do a lot to manage state information with the Scripting API. There's a ScriptState class that is returned from RunAsync() that you can use to retain information from one script execution to another. Listing 4-6 shows you how to use ScriptState to manage a script session (assume that this method is part of the Program class from the "Evaluating Scripts" section).

Listing 4-6. Using state management for scripts

```
private static async Task ExecuteScriptsWithStateAsync()
{
  Console.Out.WriteLine(
    "Enter in your script - type \"STOP\" to quit:");

  ScriptState<object> state = null;

  while (true)
  {
    var code = Console.In.ReadLine();

    if (code == "STOP")
    {
      break;
    }
```

```
    else
    {
      state = state == null ?
        await CSharpScript.RunAsync(code) :
        await state.ContinueWithAsync(code);

      foreach(var variable in state.Variables)
      {
        Console.Out.WriteLine(
          $"\t{variable.Name} - {variable.Type.Name}");
      }

      if (state.ReturnValue != null)
      {
        Console.Out.WriteLine(
          $"\tReturn value: {state.ReturnValue}");
      }
    }
  }
}
```

As long as the given text doesn't equal "STOP", the code will continue running the script. Note that we capture the return value of RunAsync() (or ContinueWithAsync() if the state already exists). This return value will contain all of the code that was parsed in previous script executions. For example, we can print out the variables that have been created from each execution. Figure 4-19 shows how variables are retained as more script is entered.

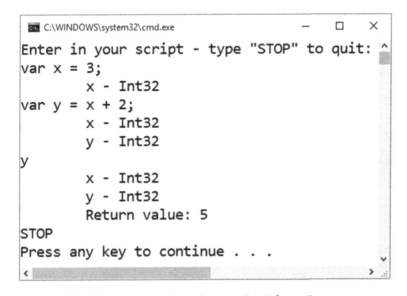

Figure 4-19. *Using state to retain script execution information*

As Figure 4-19 shows, the first line of code creates a variable called x. The next line creates a new variable y, but because we're using ScriptState, we can reference the x variable.

Keep in mind that you can always use a global context object as you saw in the code in Listing 4-4. You can also reuse that context object across different script executions. Let's say we defined a class called DictionaryContext:

```
using System.Collections.Generic;

namespace ScriptingContext
{
  public sealed class DictionaryContext
  {
    public DictionaryContext()
    {
      this.Values = new Dictionary<string, object>();
    }

    public Dictionary<string, object> Values { get; }
  }
}
```

Listing 4-7 shows how you can manage state with a DictionaryContext instance (again, this code is part of the Program class from the "Evaluating Scripts" section).

Listing 4-7. Using a shared global object to store state

```
private static async Task ExecuteScriptsWithGlobalContextAsync()
{
  Console.Out.WriteLine(
    "Enter in your script - type \"STOP\" to quit:");

  var session = new DictionaryContext();

  while (true)
  {
    var code = Console.In.ReadLine();

    if (code == "STOP")
    {
      break;
    }
    else
    {
      var result = await CSharpScript.RunAsync(code,
        globals: session);
```

```
        if(result.ReturnValue != null)
        {
          Console.Out.WriteLine(
            $"\t{result.ReturnValue}");
        }
      }
    }
  }
}
```

Figure 4-20 demonstrates how shared state, stored in DictionaryContext, can be used.

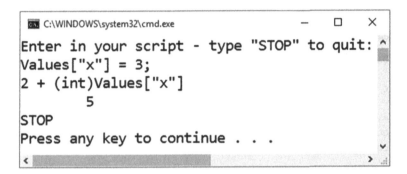

Figure 4-20. *Using a global object to share state*

We don't preserve variables between script executions, but we can store and load values from the shared context. Notice that because all of the values are stored as an object, we have to cast the value back to what we think it should be if we try to retrieve it from the dictionary.

Although we've spent a fair amount of time in this chapter looking at the cool features of the Scripting API, there are a couple of aspects of this API that you should be aware of if you decide to include its features in your applications. These are performance, memory usage, and security. Before I close out this chapter, let's take a look at these concerns in detail.

Concerns with the Scripting API

Being able to use C# as a scripting language is a welcome addition to the language's capability. However, there are a couple of areas where care should be taken to minimize potential problems from becoming actual issues. We'll discuss security later in the "Scripts and Security" section, but first we'll start with performance concerns and memory usage in scripts.

Scripts, Performance, and Memory Usage

When you see the Scripting API for the first time, you may start thinking about adding the ability to extend applications with dynamic C# code execution. As you saw with VBA in the "Orchestrating an Environment" section, exposing an object model for an application allows users to add features that aren't included within the application. However, keep in mind that there's there a cost involved with using scripts, both in performance and memory usage.

Let's create a small piece of code in a console application that will continually generate a simplistic, random C# mathematical statement and run it with the Scripting API. Once 1000 scripts are generated, it will generate the working set of the application along with how long it took to execute those scripts. Listing 4-8 shows how this works.

Listing 4-8. Executing random code via the Scripting API

```
using System.Diagnostics;

private static async Task EvaluateRandomScriptsAsync()
{
  var random = new Random();
  var iterations = 0;
  var stopWatch = Stopwatch.StartNew();

  while (true)
  {
    var script = $@"({random.Next(1000)} + {random.Next(1000)}) *
      {random.Next(10000)}";
    await CSharpScript.EvaluateAsync(script);
    iterations++;

    if (iterations == 1000)
    {
      stopWatch.Stop();
      Console.Out.WriteLine(
        $"{Environment.WorkingSet} - time: {stopWatch.Elapsed}");
      stopWatch = Stopwatch.StartNew();
      iterations = 0;
    }
  }
}
```

The code in Listing 4-8 generates code that looks like this: (452 + 112) * 34. To run this method, we'll put it into a Program class:

```
using Microsoft.CodeAnalysis.CSharp.Scripting;
using Nito.AsyncEx;
using System;
using System.Diagnostics;
```

```
using System.Linq.Expressions;
using System.Threading.Tasks;

namespace ScriptingAndMemory
{
  class Program
  {
    static void Main(string[] args)
    {
      AsyncContext.Run(
        () => Program.MainAsync(args));
    }

    private static async Task MainAsync(string[] args)
    {
      await EvaluateRandomScriptsAsync();
    }

    private static async Task EvaluateRandomScriptsAsync()
    {
      /* ... */
    }
  }
}
```

Figure 4-21 shows what happens when you run this code.

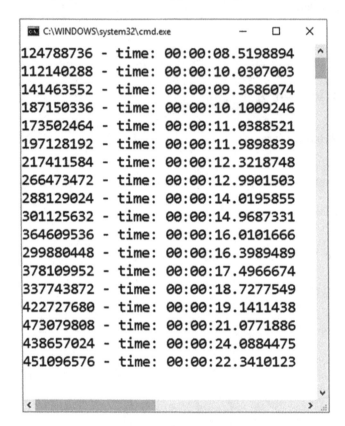

Figure 4-21. *Memory and performance characteristics of script execution*

Notice that the size of the working set slowly, but surely, increases over time. Also, the time to execute 1000 scripts slowly increases as well.

Let's compare this approach of generating and executing dynamically generated code using the Scripting API with another technique: expressions. The System.Linq.Expressions namespace has types that allow you to create methods that are compiled to IL, just like C# code. Listing 4-9 shows how the Expressions API is used to create methods that are functionally the same as the script code generated in Listing 4-9 (note that this method exists in our Program class).

Listing 4-9. Executing random code via the Expressions API

```
private static void EvaluateRandomExpressions()
{
  var random = new Random();
  var iterations = 0;
  var stopWatch = Stopwatch.StartNew();
```

```
while (true)
{
  var lambda = Expression.Lambda(
    Expression.Multiply(
      Expression.Add(
        Expression.Constant(random.Next(1000)),
        Expression.Constant(random.Next(1000))),
      Expression.Constant(random.Next(10000))));
  (lambda.Compile() as Func<int>)();
  iterations++;

  if (iterations == 1000)
  {
    stopWatch.Stop();
    Console.Out.WriteLine(
      $"{Environment.WorkingSet} - time: {stopWatch.Elapsed}");
    stopWatch = Stopwatch.StartNew();
    iterations = 0;
  }
}
}
```

Figure 4-22 shows the performance characteristics of the Expressions API approach by calling EvaluateRandomExpressions() from the Program's Main() method.

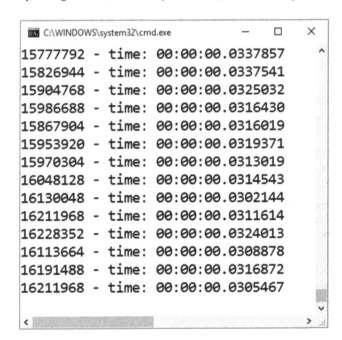

Figure 4-22. Memory and performance characteristics of expression execution

In this case, the working set size and performance values are stable. The working set size is also smaller than the Scripting API approach. Furthermore, based on the values generated by this code, the Expressions API approach is three orders of magnitude faster than the Scripting API. For example, a script takes about 0.015 seconds to run. With an expression, it takes 0.00003 seconds.

The benefits of using the Expressions API doesn't mean that you should avoid using the Scripting API; far from it! Keep in mind that this test is literally creating thousands of scripts, and that's typically not how scripts are executed. Scripts are used to orchestrate other pieces of code in an application in a way that the developers didn't initially anticipate. Running a script 1000 times a second continuously within this context isn't common. Scripts are also exploratory, especially with a REPL. Once a developer has done enough C# scripting experimentation, that code can potentially be moved into a more typical compilation pipeline where the result is an assembly that can be optimized in numerous ways. Finally, a script can allow you to create new classes; the Expressions API is limited to a method implementation.

Another area where a developer should be cautious with scripts is with security. Let's investigate this issue next.

Scripts and Security

It's tempting to give users the ability to interact with an application's features in ways that were not originally codified as pieces of accepted functionality. For example, I've seen a number of applications at clients that I've consulted for where users can create reports based on the information contained within the application's database. Usually, this means they can submit SQL statements and save the data into an Excel spreadsheet. Initially, this sounds like a great idea, because the application empowers uses to go beyond what the application can provide. Unfortunately, this can also be a source of unexpected problems as well, such as:

- Performance. Queries that are submitted may cause significant delays due to unexpected fields being seached, where those fields do not have any indexes in place. This can affect the performance of other areas of the application.

- Resource use. If the users enter queries that start with "SELECT *", they may retrieve a large amount of data that will tax the system's resources.

- Security. Entering queries that take advantage of SQL injection techniques may cause significant damage to the data contained within the database.

Security is the issue we'll focus on. If you want to use the Scripting API, you have to keep in mind what functionality the user will have available and ensure they can only use certain .NET members in their script code, or prevent them from using potentially harmful APIs. Let's look at an example.

This demonstration uses a console application that provides an object model for a user to interact with. The first step is to create a simple Person class defined as follows:

```
public sealed class Person
{
  public Person(string name, uint age)
  {
    this.Name = name;
    this.Age = age;
  }

  public void Save() { }

  public uint Age { get; set; }
  public string Name { get; set; }
}
```

We'll also create a script context that exposes a list of people:

```
public sealed class ScriptingContext
{
  public ScriptingContext()
  {
    this.People = ImmutableArray.Create(
      new Person("Joe Smith", 30),
      new Person("Daniel Davis", 20),
      new Person("Sofia Wright", 25));
  }

  public ImmutableArray<Person> People { get; }
}
```

This is the object model that we'll pass to the CSharpScript class so scripts can query the list and find people that match a set of criteria the user defines. Listing 4-10 shows the asynchronous MainAsync() method that is created to handle this scenario.

Listing 4-10. Running scripts with an accesssible application object model

```
using System.IO;
using System.Linq;

private static async Task MainAsync(string[] args)
{
  File.WriteAllLines("secrets.txt",
    new[] { "Secret password: 12345" });

  Console.Out.WriteLine(
    "Enter in your script - type \"STOP\" to quit:");
```

```
var context = new ScriptingContext();
var options = ScriptOptions.Default
  .AddImports(
    typeof(ImmutableArrayExtensions).Namespace)
  .AddReferences(
    typeof(ImmutableArrayExtensions).Assembly);

while (true)
{
  var code = Console.In.ReadLine();

  if (code == "STOP")
  {
    break;
  }
  else
  {
    var script = CSharpScript.Create(code,
      globalsType: typeof(ScriptingContext),
      options: options);
    var compilation = script.GetCompilation();
    var diagnostics = compilation.GetDiagnostics();

    if (diagnostics.Length > 0)
    {
      foreach (var diagnostic in diagnostics)
      {
        Console.Out.WriteLine(diagnostic);
      }
    }
    else
    {
      var result = await CSharpScript.RunAsync(code,
        globals: context,
        options: options);

      if(result.ReturnValue != null)
      {
        Console.Out.WriteLine($"\t{result.ReturnValue}");
      }
    }
  }
}
}
```

The code is similar to code you saw in Listing 4-5. We create a global context object so scripts can use members on that context. If there are no errors, we run the script. Figure 4-23 shows what happens when a script is entered that uses LINQ to query the People array.

Figure 4-23. *Running a script to find specific people*

As expected, looking for people with a name that starts with "Joe" returns one person. But notice that MainAsync() creates a file with secret information when it starts. If a script user started using members from the System.IO namespace like this:

```
System.IO.Directory.EnumerateFiles(".").ToList()
  .ForEach(_ => System.Console.Out.WriteLine(_));
```

They'll see "secrets.txt" in the resulting list printed out to the Console window. Figure 4-24 shows the harm that can be done with this information.

```
C:\WINDOWS\system32\cmd.exe                            —    □    ×
Enter in your script - type "STOP" to quit:
System.IO.File.ReadAllLines("secrets.txt")[0]
         Secret password: 12345
STOP
Press any key to continue . . .
```

Figure 4-24. *Finding secrets in a scripting session*

This isn't good! With a small amount of code, a user can find files of interest, and then read that file's contents. Or, a malicious user could use System.IO types to delete numerous files on the hard drive.

133

We definitely do not want users to have access to the file system in this application. Therefore, we should prevent usage of anything from the System.IO namespace. However, that's not sufficient. Consider this line of code:

```
System.Type.GetType("System.IO.File").GetMethod(
  "ReadAllLines", new[] { typeof(string) }).Invoke(null, new[] { "secrets.txt" });
```

This code never uses any System.IO type or member directly. Rather, it uses the Reflection API to make a method call that will read file contents. If we were specifically looking for System.IO usage, this would circumvent it. Therefore, we definitely want to stop any Reflection API usage.

But there's potentially one more issue at hand. Take a look at this script snippet:

```
var person = People.Where(_ => _.Name.StartsWith("Joe"))
  .ToArray()[0]; person.Name = "Changed Name"; person.Save();
```

Do we want users to have the ability to change a person's name, along with calling Save()? Granted, Save() doesn't do anything in our example, but it's easy to imagine a real-world example where Save() may try to access a database and persist any changes. Maybe the user won't have that kind of authority with their account's permissions, but we can also prevent scripts that try to persist changes on a Person instance from being executed in the first place.

To implement all the security restrictions we just discussed, we'll create a VerifyCompilation() method that will traverse nodes in the syntax tree from the script and examine whether any undesirable members are being used in that code. Listing 4-11 shows how VerifyCompilation() is defined.

Listing 4-11. Analyzing scripts for invalid member usage

```
private static ImmutableArray<Diagnostic> VerifyCompilation(
  Compilation compilation)
{
  var diagnostics = new List<Diagnostic>();

  foreach (var tree in compilation.SyntaxTrees)
  {
    var model = compilation.GetSemanticModel(tree);
    foreach (var node in tree.GetRoot().DescendantNodes(
      _ => true))
    {
      var symbol = model.GetSymbolInfo(node).Symbol;

      if (symbol != null)
      {
        var symbolNamespace = Program.GetFullNamespace(symbol);
```

```
    if(symbol.Kind == SymbolKind.Method ||
      symbol.Kind == SymbolKind.Property ||
      symbol.Kind == SymbolKind.NamedType)
    {
      if(symbol.Kind == SymbolKind.Method)
      {
        if (symbolNamespace == typeof(Person).Namespace &&
          symbol.ContainingType.Name == nameof(Person) &&
          symbol.Name == nameof(Person.Save))
        {
          diagnostics.Add(Diagnostic.Create(
            new DiagnosticDescriptor("SCRIPT02",
              "Persistence Error", "Cannot save a person",
              "Usage", DiagnosticSeverity.Error, false),
            node.GetLocation()));
        }
      }

      if (symbolNamespace == "System.IO" ||
        symbolNamespace == "System.Reflection")
      {
        diagnostics.Add(Diagnostic.Create(
          new DiagnosticDescriptor("SCRIPT01",
            "Inaccessable Member",
            "Cannot allow a member from namespace {0} to be used",
            "Usage", DiagnosticSeverity.Error, false),
          node.GetLocation(), symbolNamespace));
      }
    }
  }
 }
}

  return diagnostics.ToImmutableArray();
}
```

We attempt to get an ISymbol reference for every node in the syntax tree. If we come across a method, property, or type, we look for two conditions. The first one is when the symbol reference is actually a call to Save() on a Person object. The other one is when the symbol exists within either the System.IO or the System.Reflection namespace. The GetFullNamespace() method gets us the namespace of the symbol; here's how GetFullNamespace() is implemented:

```
private static string GetFullNamespace(ISymbol symbol)
{
  var namespaces = new List<string>();
  var @namespace = symbol.ContainingNamespace;
```

```
while(@namespace != null)
{
  if(!string.IsNullOrWhiteSpace(@namespace.Name))
  {
    namespaces.Add(@namespace.Name);
  }

  @namespace = @namespace.ContainingNamespace;
}

namespaces.Reverse();

return string.Join(".", namespaces);
}
```

With VerifyImplementation() in place, we need to change only one line of code in MainAsync(). Change this line:

```
var diagnostics = compilation.GetDiagnostics();
```

To this:

```
var diagnostics = compilation.GetDiagnostics()
  .Union(Program.VerifyCompilation(
    compilation))
  .ToImmutableArray();
```

This code combines the diagnostic results from the compilation of the script with any custom diagnostics generated from our analysis.

Now, let's run a couple of tests against this new implementation. First, let's run a script that tries to modify and save a Person instance. Figure 4-25 shows you what happens.

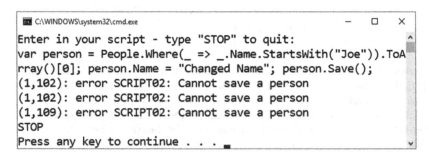

Figure 4-25. *Preventing persistence on a Person object*

As expected, the script isn't executed and we get an error. Figure 4-26 shows similar behavior when we try to use Reflection to read secret information in a file.

```
C:\WINDOWS\system32\cmd.exe                                    —    □    ×
Enter in your script - type "STOP" to quit:
System.Type.GetType("System.IO.File").GetMethod("ReadAllLine
s", new[] { typeof(string) }).Invoke(null, new[] { "secrets.
txt" });
(1,1): error SCRIPT01: Cannot allow a member from namespace
System.Reflection to be used
(1,1): error SCRIPT01: Cannot allow a member from namespace
System.Reflection to be used
(1,91): error SCRIPT01: Cannot allow a member from namespace
 System.Reflection to be used
STOP
Press any key to continue . . .
```

Figure 4-26. *Preventing Reflection calls in a script*

These security-based techniques should be kept in mind if you let users write C# scripts in your applications. However, realize that these security measures don't cover all of the bases. Here are some other thoughts to consider:

- API Exclusion. There may be more APIs that you'll need to blacklist to prevent malicious activites from being executed. For example, we don't prevent members from System.Reflection.Emit from being used here. You'd definitely want to include those members because a user could write script that literally creates a new assembly on the fly.

- Restricted UIs. Our example used a simple console application. Real-world applications that users interact with are typically web-, mobile-, or desktop-based. You can create a UI that allows users to interact with the object model but in a restricted way. For example, you can provide a drop down that allows the user to query the People list with standardized actions, like "Starts with" for the name, and "less than" for the age. The user doesn't enter code; they interact with UI elements whose values are used to generate script. However, this may limit the ability for the user to interact with the application's object model in ways you can't anticipate.

- Use Restricted User Accounts. Ensure that the identity that is used to execute the script is highly limited. For example, you can create a user account that cannot interact with files on the machine where the script is executed. This would prevent the script from being able to use files even if malicious users figured out how to write script to get around the prevention techniques demonstrated in this section.

Trying to limit what a script can do is not a trivial endeavour. With flexibility and extensibility comes responsibilty and governance. You must ensure that exposing script execution in an application does not reveal any security holes for users to take advantage of.

Conclusion

In this chapter, you saw how you can treat C# as a scripting language with the Scripting API. This included using the Interactive window in Visual Studio and using the CSharpScript object to compile and execute script. Performance and security considerations with C# as a scripting language were also investigated. In the next and final chapter, you'll learn how the Compiler API is already being used by open source packages and how C# may change in the future using the Compiler API's features.

CHAPTER 5

The Future of the Compiler API

Although this is the last chapter in this book, the story of the Compiler API doesn't end. What does the future hold for the Compiler API? To close out this book, we'll look at tools and frameworks that are already taking advantage of the Compiler API in creative and versatile ways. We'll also explore the upcoming possible transformation of C# with metaprogramming and code injection.

Current Usage

Throughout this book, you saw how the Compiler API is used to enable a developer to write diagnostics and refactorings, along with the Scripting API that makes C# into a scripting language. Although these are powerful capabilities that provide a developer with rich information about their code, there is no limitation in terms of where you can use these API sets in your C# code. You can include the Compiler API packages and tools that are taking advantage of the Compiler API into your own projects via NuGet. We'll take a look at packages that user the Compiler API in this section, starting with a mocking framework I created called Rocks.

Generating Mocks

If you've ever done any unit testing in .NET, you've probably come across the need or desire to create "fake" versions of dependencies. Let's use a very generic example to illustrate this. Let's say you have a class that uses a dependency based on an interface called IService:

```
public interface IService
{
  int GetId();
}
```

There's a class called ServiceUser that uses an implementation of the service to get an ID value:

```
public sealed class ServiceUser
{
  public ServiceUser(IService service)
  {
    if(service == null)
    {
      throw new ArgumentNullException(nameof(service));
    }

    this.Id = service.GetId();
  }

  public int Id { get; }
}
```

This is an example of dependency injection. The ServiceUser class needs to use an object that implements IService, but it doesn't care what that object does to get the ID value. It could be calling a REST service, it could be reading a file, or it could be accessing a database: the point is, ServiceUser doesn't care. It only needs to call GetId().

Now, to test ServiceUser, we need an instance of IService. But we don't necessarily want to talk to the object that will be used at runtime during the unit test due to concerns like performance and isolation. For example, if the implementation is talking to a service, latency time may creep into the test along with other tests that need to use the dependency. In addition, we're testing ServiceUser; we're not testing how the implementation of IService works. Focusing our testing responsibilities on the code we want to test is essential.

A typical approach during a test is to create a mock object. This is an object that implements a given abstraction (like an interface), but it also allows the developer to specify expectations. That is, the developer can state the behaviors and interactions that should occur with the mock during the test run. There are great frameworks that already exist in the .NET space that create mocks, such as Moq (http://www.moqthis.com) and NSubstitute (http://nsubstitute.github.io). Listing 5-1 shows how you can run code that will test ServiceUser's interaction with a mock of IService.

Listing 5-1. Using Moq to create a mock object

```
using Moq;

private static void MockUsingMoq()
{
  var service = new Mock<IService>(MockBehavior.Strict);
  service.Setup(_ => _.GetId()).Returns(2);
```

```
    var user = new ServiceUser(service.Object);
    Debug.Assert(user.Id == 2);

    service.VerifyAll();
}
```

The Mock class allows the developer to create an expectation that GetId() will be called via Setup(). Since this method returns a value, Returns() is used to specify that the value 2 will be returned. Debug.Assert() checks that the Id property is equal to 2, which should have been set from the GetId() call. Finally, VerifyAll() is called on the mock to ensure that all expectations were satisfied.

However, there's one architecture issue with frameworks like Moq and NSubstitute. A mocking framework needs to synthesize a new class at runtime based on the abstraction that it's given. To do this, the mocking framework typically use members from the System.Reflection.Emit namespace, which allows you to create a class on the fly. The issue with this namespace is that you have to know how IL works in .NET. IL is the language that any language that wants to run on .NET must compile to. While it's not as difficult as pure x86 assembly language, as mentioned in the "What Do Compilers Do?" section in Chapter 1, it's not trivial either. IL is not a language most .NET developers know, and even if they've spent time in it, it's very easy to create code via IL that fails in ways that have never been seen before. What we need is a better way to create code on the fly in a language that most .NET developers know. And that's exactly what the Compiler API gives us and the reason I created Rocks (https://github.com/jasonbock/rocks). Rocks is a mocking framework that's similar to Moq and NSubstitute but has one key difference: it uses the Compiler API to create a class at runtime rather than IL. To a developer using Rocks, it doesn't seem much different than other .NET mocking frameworks. Listing 5-2 shows how to create a mock object using the same code from Listing 5-1 except instead of using Moq it uses Rocks.

Listing 5-2. Using Rocks to create a mock object

```
using Rocks;
using Rocks.Options;

private static void MockUsingRocks()
{
    var service = Rock.Create<IService>();
    service.Handle(_ => _.GetId()).Returns(2);

    var user = new ServiceUser(service.Make());
    Debug.Assert(user.Id == 2);

    service.Verify();
}
```

But the mock generated when Make() is called is based on pure C# code. To see this, change the line of code with Rock.Create() from this:

```
var service = Rock.Create<IService>();
```

to this:

```
var service = Rock.Create<IService>(
  new RockOptions(
    level: OptimizationSetting.Debug,
    codeFile: CodeFileOptions.Create));
```

Then, put a breakpoint on the line of code that creates a new instance of ServiceUser, and start Visual Studio in Debug mode. When the breakpoint is hit, press F11, which will step into the implementation of the mock. You should see a screen in Visual Studio similar to Figure 5-1.

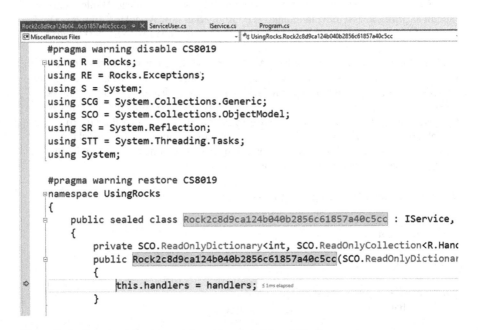

Figure 5-1. *Stepping into generated mock code in Visual Studio*

Note that the generated class uses a Guid in its name to prevent any kind of name collision with other types. The class also inherits from IService, so any code that needs to interact with an IService interface (like ServiceUser) can use this mock.

What's amazing about creating mocks using the Compiler API is that the Compiler API makes it extremely simple to debug dynamic code generated at runtime based on how the Compiler API is supposed to work in the first place! Rocks takes advantage of the fact that you can compile code with debug symbols generated. There's very little Rocks

has to do to implement debugging capabilities. If you want to do this with types from
System.Reflection.Emit, well, it's a long story, but it's difficult. You have to manually
generate an .il file yourself and match up all the lines of code to debug symbols manually.
A Rocks user will probably never step into the generated mock code, but for me as the
implementor of Rocks, it's been a great feature to take advantage of when I'm trying to
diagnose issues with my mock code generation.

Creating mocks is one area where you can take advantage of the Compiler API's ability to
generate code. Let's look at another innovate package that helps you target the Web with C#.

Building Code with Code

Ever since .NET's inception, MSBuild has been the standard way to build code. MSBuild
understands solutions and projects and can orchestrate their builds as well as provide
customizations to the process, such as running tests and deploying binaries. However,
MSBuild is not the only way to build code. A vast array of build tools and scripting
languages are available to use for your building concerns. One tool is called Cake
(http://cakebuild.net/), which uses the Compiler API to execute build steps using
a C#-like domain specific language (DSL). Let's create a solution that has two projects
to see how we can use Cake to handle the build steps. One project is a class library
called RandomGeneration that uses a NuGet package to generate a random number, and
the other project called RandomGeneration.Tests has tests for our class library. The
RandomGeneration project will also have a .nuspec file that can be used to generate a
NuGet package.

Here's what the Randomness class looks like (which exists in RandomGeneration):

```
using Spackle;

namespace RandomGeneration
{
  public sealed class Randomness
  {
    public int GetValue(int start, int end)
    {
      return new SecureRandom().Next(start, end);
    }
  }
}
```

The SecureRandom class comes from a NuGet package I've created called Spackle
(https://www.nuget.org/packages/Spackle/). Speaking of NuGet, here's what the
RandomGeneration.nuspec file looks like for this project:

```
<?xml version="1.0" encoding="utf-8"?>
<package>
  <metadata>
    <id>RandomGeneration</id>
    <version>1.0.0</version>
```

```
      <authors>Jason Bock</authors>
      <owners>Jason Bock</owners>
      <description>Generate random numbers within a range.</description>
      <tags>netframework</tags>
      <language>en-US</language>
      <dependencies>
         <dependency id="Spackle" version="7.1.0" />
      </dependencies>
   </metadata>
   <files>
      <file src="RandomGeneration.dll" target="lib\net46" />
   </files>
</package>
```

Here's the code that tests GetValue():

```
using Microsoft.VisualStudio.TestTools.UnitTesting;

namespace RandomGeneration.Tests
{
  [TestClass]
  public sealed class RandomnessTests
  {
    [TestMethod]
    public void GetValue()
    {
      var value = new Randomness().GetValue(2, 10);
      Assert.IsTrue(value >= 2);
      Assert.IsTrue(value <= 10);
    }
  }
}
```

Now, let's see how we can get Cake involved in the build process. Here are the steps we want to perform:

1. Build the RandomGeneration class library.

2. Run the tests in RandomGeneration.Tests.

3. Create a NuGet package file based on the RandomGeneration.
    nuspec definition.

The first action is to create a Cake bootstrapper file. This boostrapper file is a PowerShell script that will run our Cake build file. To make this file, open a PowerShell window, navigate to the directory that contains the RandomGeneration solution file, and run the following command:

```
Invoke-WebRequest http://cakebuild.net/bootstrapper/windows -OutFile build.ps1
```

You should get a build.ps1 file in your solution directory when this is done. Now, you need to create a cake.build file in this directory. The cake.build file is just a text file so you can use any text editor you want to create it. Listing 5-3 shows what the build file looks like for our RandomGeneration solution.

Listing 5-3. Definition of the Cake build file

```
var target = Argument<string>("target", "Default");
var configuration = Argument<string>("configuration", "Release");
var solution = "RandomGeneration.sln";

Task("Clean")
  .Does(() =>
  {
    CleanDirectories("./**/bin/" + configuration);
    CleanDirectories("./**/obj/" + configuration);
  });

Task("Restore")
  .Does(() =>
  {
    NuGetRestore(solution);
  });

Task("Build")
  .IsDependentOn("Clean")
  .IsDependentOn("Restore")
  .Does(() =>
  {
    MSBuild(solution, settings =>
      settings.SetPlatformTarget(PlatformTarget.MSIL)
        .WithTarget("Build")
        .SetConfiguration(configuration));
  });

Task("Tests")
  .IsDependentOn("Build")
  .Does(() =>
  {
    MSTest("./**/*.Tests.dll",
      new MSTestSettings
      {
        NoIsolation = true
      });
  });
```

```
Task("NuGetPack")
  .IsDependentOn("Tests")
  .Does(() =>
  {
    CreateDirectory("./NuGet Pack");
    CopyFile("./RandomGeneration/RandomGeneration.nuspec",
      "./NuGet Pack/RandomGeneration.nuspec");
    CopyDirectory("./RandomGeneration/bin/Release",
      "./NuGet Pack");
    NuGetPack("./NuGet Pack/RandomGeneration.nuspec",
      new NuGetPackSettings
      {
        OutputDirectory = "./NuGet Pack"
      });
  });

Task("Default")
  .IsDependentOn("Build")
  .IsDependentOn("Tests")
  .IsDependentOn("NuGetPack");

RunTarget(target);
```

Although it may look like a lot of code, it's pretty easy to decipher a Cake script. You define tasks that should be run during a build with the Task() method. Tasks can have dependencies on other tasks—for example, in this script, the "Clean" and "Restore" tasks must execute before the "Build" task runs. Each task can execute code in the Does() action method. It's completely up to you to do what you think is necessary for each task. For example, in the "Build" task, the MSBuild() method is used to build all the code in the solution. The "Tests" task runs all of the tests via the MSTest() method. Also, keep in mind that Cake is smart enough to run each task only once, even if tasks are declared as dependencies more than once.

Once you have the script file setup, you run "./build.ps1" in a PowerShell command window. This script will get the necessary Cake components if it can't find them, and then the build.ps1 script will build your Cake script file. This is where the power of the Compiler API comes into play. Because your Cake script file is really C# code, you can write your build process in the language you code in. You can declare variables and use other .NET libraries—it's completely up to you. Once the code is compiled, Cake runs the default task.

■ **Note**   You'll find a number of built-in Cake tasks and methods at http://cakebuild. net/dsl. Also, you can create your own aliases to extend the build process: you'll find the details at http://cakebuild.net/docs/fundamentals/aliases. Additionally, there are numerous add-ins you can use to control other tools, such as AppVeyor, Slack, and HockeyApp; this list is at http://cakebuild.net/api.

If you haven't set up a build server or done automated deployments, I highly recommend you consider using a tool like Cake to do it. Automating manual steps leads to greater productivity, and the Compiler API can empower your continuous integration and deployment needs.

Other Compiler API-Based Tools and Frameworks

The Rocks and Cake packages you saw earlier are just a small sample of what's already available in the .NET space that use the Compiler API. Here are some other packages you should check out:

- DotNetAnalyzers (https://github.com/DotNetAnalyzers/DotNetAnalyzers) and StyleCopAnalyzers (https://github.com/DotNetAnalyzers/StyleCopAnalyzers)—a suite of diagnostics that enforce rules partially based on the StyleCop tool (http://stylecop.codeplex.com/).

- ScriptCS (http://scriptcs.net/)—a C# scripting implementation

- OmniSharp (http://www.omnisharp.net/)—a .NET editor written entirely in .NET

- RefactoringEssentials (http://vsrefactoringessentials.com/)—a suite of refactorings and analyzers

- ConfigR (https://github.com/config-r/config-r)—a package that uses C# code to power configuration files

This list is not exhaustive by any means. .NET code is being infused with the power of the Compiler API. More and more tools and packages are using its capabilities to power their features. But, what about the C# language itself? In the next section, you'll examine how the Compiler API may affect the fundamental way you write code in C#.

Looking into C#'s Future

It's great to see open-source packages use the Compiler API in innovative and creative ways. But wouldn't it be ideal to share pieces of code in .NET to greatly simplify applications? Can we change how C# works so code generation is an integral part of the language? There are strong hints that the next version of C# will have this capability. To close out this chapter, let's take a theoretical look at how source generators will affect the way you code in C# in a deep, revolutionary way.

■ **Note** Keep in mind that this source generator feature is still experimental at the time of this writing, so I won't go into any specifics on its implementation. It was demonstrated at //BUILD (https://channel9.msdn.com/Events/Build/2016/B889—start watching at the 54:00 mark), and two GitHub issues are related to this feature at https://github.com/dotnet/roslyn/issues/5561 and https://github.com/dotnet/roslyn/issues/5292; related issues are tagged with "New Language Feature—Replace/Original." In addition, it's in C#7's "strong interest" section for proposed features (https://github.com/dotnet/roslyn/issues/2136). That said, there is no guarantee that source generators will be in the next version of C#, but it's a feature that C# developers should be watching because it has the potential to radically change how they design their applications.

A Quick Story About Property Change Notifications

One example of what .NET developers have been begging for in an automatic implementation of a specific scenario is property change notification. A property change notification happens when your class implements INotifyPropertyChanged. Here's one way you can implement this interface. You create a base class that implements INotifyPropertyChanged, as shown in Listing 5-4.

Listing 5-4. Providing a reusable implementation of INotifyPropertyChanged

```
public abstract class Properties
  : INotifyPropertyChanged
{
  public event PropertyChangedEventHandler PropertyChanged;

  protected Properties() { }

  protected virtual void OnPropertyChanged(string propertyName)
  {
    this.PropertyChanged?.Invoke(this,
      new PropertyChangedEventArgs(propertyName));
  }

  protected void SetField<T>(ref T field,
    T value, string propertyName)
  {
    if (!EqualityComparer<T>.Default.Equals(field, value))
    {
      field = value;
      this.OnPropertyChanged(propertyName);
    }
  }
}
```

Then, you can inherit from the Properties class to publish property change events:

```
public class IntegerData
  : Properties
{
  private int value;
  public int Value
  {
    get { return this.value; }
    set { this.SetField(ref this.value, value, nameof(Value)); }
  }
}
```

If you use the code from Listing 5-4 and the IntegerData class in a console application like this, you change the Value property to different values:

```
private static void Main()
{
  var properties = new IntegerData();
  properties.PropertyChanged +=
    (s, e) => Console.Out.WriteLine(
      $"Property {e.PropertyName} changed.");
  Console.Out.WriteLine(
    $"properties.Value is {properties.Value}");
  properties.Value = 2;
  Console.Out.WriteLine(
    $"properties.Value is {properties.Value}");
  properties.Value = 3;
  Console.Out.WriteLine(
    $"properties.Value is {properties.Value}");
  properties.Value = 3;
  Console.Out.WriteLine(
    $"properties.Value is {properties.Value}");
  properties.Value = 4;
  Console.Out.WriteLine(
    $"properties.Value is {properties.Value}");
}
```

Figure 5-2 shows what happens.

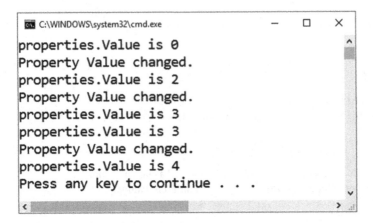

Figure 5-2. *Receiving property change notifications*

As expected, you only get property change notifications when the property value actually changes.

Although this code works as expected, the result isn't ideal. One problem with this approach of using a base class is that a developer cannot use inheritance effectively. Because you can only inherit from one class, you can't inherit from any other classes other than Properties. However, if you don't provide a base class that handles INotifyPropertyChanged, you force *every* class that wants to do change notifications to implement INotifyPropertyChanged. There are ways to get around this issue of single class inheritance as well, but none of them solve the problem elegantly. The C# language could address this by adding a new keyword like "notify" that a developer could use on properties. The C# compiler would then be responsible for generating the property changed code machinery. But, this solution isn't scalable. There are numerous cases where coding aspects like implementing INotifyPropertyChanged should be handled in a repeatable fashion. We can't create keywords every time we run into conditions where we want to repeat an implementation of code in numerous places of an application.

In the next section, I'll talk about how repeatable code generation scenarios may be improved in a future version of C#.

Reusing Common Implementations

A better approach to handling INotifyPropertyChanged is to provide a common, reusable approach independent of keywords and typical code reuse techniques. The following code snippet shows what a developer would want to do:

```
[PropertyChanged]
public partial class IntegerData
{
  public int Value { get; set;}
}
```

The idea here is that the C# compiler would see the PropertyChangedAttribute and use the attribute's implementation to generate code for the target class, correctly implementing INotifyPropertyChanged. These attributes would be different than the attributes that we currently create in that these compile-time attributes wouldn't be passive. The compiler would look for their presence and inform them to generate code to augment the code that they are tied to. In the case of this hypothetical PropertyChangedAttribute, it would ensure the target class would implement INotifyPropertyChanged and implement the property changed logic within each property setter. This technique is a huge win for developers because they no longer have to manually write that code; the attribute will generate it for them!

But, let's not stop with property changed notifications. Consider a scenario in which we have a class that implements IDisposable along with overriding ToString() and defining a method, which is shown in Listing 5-5.

Listing 5-5. Defining a class with embedded, reusable implementations

```
public class Person
  : IDisposable
{
  private bool isDisposed;
  private int disposedCallCount;
  private int callTwiceCallCount;

  public Person(string name, uint age)
  {
    this.Name = name;
    this.Age = age;
  }

  public string Name { get; }
  public uint Age { get; }

  public override string ToString()
  {
    if(this.isDisposed)
    {
      throw new ObjectDisposedExcecption(nameof(Person));
    }

    return $"{this.Name}, {this.Age}";
  }

  public void Dispose()
  {
    if(this.isDisposed)
    {
      throw new ObjectDisposedExcecption(nameof(Person));
    }
```

```
    if(Interlocked.Increment(ref this.disposedCallCount) > 1)
    {
      throw new MaximumCallCountExceededException(nameof(Dispose));
    }

    // Do all the nasty gunk that you need
    // to do to support Dispose()...
  }

  public void CallTwice()
  {
    if(this.isDisposed)
    {
      throw new ObjectDisposedExcecption(nameof(Person));
    }

    if(Interlocked.Increment(ref this.callTwiceCallCount) > 2)
    {
      throw new MaximumCallCountExceededException(nameof(CallTwice));
    }

    // Do what CallTwice() does...
  }
}
```

For a simple class, there's a fair amount of code in place that isn't specific to the Person class, such as:

- Object disposal. The IDisposable interface requires a number of steps that developers should follow to implement the idiom correctly (see https://msdn.microsoft.com/en-us/library/ms244737.aspx for details). Also, each member on a disposable object should throw ObjectDisposedException if the object has been disposed.

- Method call thresholds. Sometimes a method should only be called a certain number of times. A typical scenario is Dispose(), which should only be called once. In this class, CallTwice() should only be invoked twice.

- ToString() patterns. You may want to have a consistent format for ToString() for all of your classes, like the property values concatenated together with a comma and space delimiter.

Now, compare the code in Listing 5-5 to the code in Listing 5-6.

Listing 5-6. Using generators in C# code

```
[Disposable]
[ToString]
public partial class Person
{
  public Person(string name, uint age)
  {
    this.Name = name;
    this.Age = age;
  }

  public string Name { get; }
  public uint Age { get; }

  [Throttle(2)]
  public void CallTwice()
  {
    // Do what CallTwice() does...
  }
}
```

The idea is that we'd use source generators to implement IDisposable on the class for us. We'd also implement ToString() for the developer based on a consistent, idiomatic pattern. Finally, we can throttle the number of times a method is called.

The ability to weave code into existing code via compile-time attributes will drastically reduce the amount of code a developer has to write in every class. Additionally, the implementation of a source generator would produce C# code that can be analyzed and debugged as easily as the code you wrote. The generator would use syntax trees and semantic information to determine the structure of the code and subseqently augment the tree so it contains the correct implementation. Now that you've read this book and have a solid understanding of the components of the Compiler API, you should be comfortable creating source generators for your applications.

Conclusion

This chapter showed you how tools and frameworks are already taking advantage of the Compiler API to build amazing products. Packages such as Rocks and Cake are empowered by the Compiler API to implement features that were difficult before it was introduced. You also got a glimpse into C#'s future where the Compiler API is used to allow developers to generate code so patterns and aspects can be exploited to simplify implementations.

And although you've come to the end of the book, the story of the Compiler API doesn't stop here. .NET started a major transformation that was initialized in the late 2000s when hints and small demos were given by Microsoft employees of a new world with an accessible API to the internals of the compiler. This transformation was greatly accelerated when Roslyn was open-sourced in 2014. Now, the .NET community is thriving once again. The .NET Framework is being reimaged and rearchitected into .NET Core, a nimbler, performance-driven, open-source, cross-platform version of .NET that is evolving along with the compilation framework. Furthermore, there are even hints that .NET will target WebAssembly in the future, making C# work natively in the browser (see `https://www.reddit.com/r/programmerchat/comments/4dxpcp/i_am_miguel_de_icaza_i_started_xamarin_mono_gnome/d1v9xyd`). The cool thing about all this work is that anyone can contribute to this effort. I hope that you not only consider writing your own diagnostics and refactorings along with using the Compiler and Scripting API to empower your applications, but also consider contributing to the continual evolution of the framework. Once again, it's a great time to be a .NET developer!

Index

A

AdHocWorksapce, 90, 93
AnalyzeMethodDeclaration()
    method, 41–42
Analyzer with Code Fix (NuGet + VSIX), 37
ApplyChangesOperation, 89

B

base.BaseMethod(), 47–48
BaseExpression() provides, 47

C

Cake build file, 145
CancellationToken, 60
C# interactive, scripting API
    analyzing scripts, 119–121
    NuGet package, 115
    scripts evaluation
        AddImports(), 118
        AddReferences(), 118
        CompilationErrorException, 117
        Context class, 118
        CSharpScript, 117
        CustomContext, 118–119
        custom types, 118
        EvaluateAsync(), 116–117, 119
        EvaluateCodeWith
          GlobalContextAsync(), 119
        global context object, 119
        ScriptOptions, 117
    state management, scripts, 122–125
C# interactive window
    class creation, 112
    code creation, script, 113–114
    defined classes, 112

experience, command line, 113
#help command, 111
resetting, interactive session, 111
simple calculations, 109
string, 110
variable, printing, 110
ClassDeclaractionSyntax node, 14
ClassDeclarationNode, 30
ClassDeclarationSyntax, 15
CodeRefactoringProvider, 76
CommentRemover class, 95, 99, 106
CommentRemover.ConsoleApplication.
    IntegrationTests, 100
CommentRemover—RemoveComments
    FromSolutionAsync(), 98
CommentRemover.Task project, 102
Common Language Runtime (CLR), 3
CompilationUnit, 16
CompilationUnitSyntax object, 18–19, 82
CompilationUnitSytnax node, 98
Compiler API
    annotations, 29
    assemblies, 6
    building trees, 17–20
    closed box, 4–5
    code build
        cake bootstrapper file, 144
        cake build file, 145–146
        Does() action method, 146
        MSBuild() method, 146
        RandomGeneration
          solution, 143–145
        SecureRandom class, 143
        Spackle, 143
        Task() method, 146
    compiling code
        building, 8–10
        referencing assemblies, 6, 8

Get the eBook for only $5!

Why limit yourself?

Now you can take the weightless companion with you wherever you go and access your content on your PC, phone, tablet, or reader.

Since you've purchased this print book, we're happy to offer you the eBook in all 3 formats for just $5.

Convenient and fully searchable, the PDF version enables you to easily find and copy code—or perform examples by quickly toggling between instructions and applications. The MOBI format is ideal for your Kindle, while the ePUB can be utilized on a variety of mobile devices.

To learn more, go to www.apress.com/companion or contact support@apress.com.

Printed in the United States
By Bookmasters